The Complete Rice Cooker Cookbook

Martha Williams

Introduction 1

Rice Cooker Fundamentals 3

How Rice Cookers Work 3

Types of Rice Cookers You Can Buy 3

Know The Ingredietns 6

A Few Tips For Success With Your Rice Cooker 9

Basic Rice Recipes..10

Applesauce...10

Barley 11

Brown Rice 12

Bulgur...12

Bulgur Breakfast Porridge 13

Dried Beans 14

Farro...14

Grits 15

Long-Grain Rice 16

Medium-Grain Rice 17

Oatmeal 18

Polenta 19

Quinoa 19

Short-Grain Rice 20

Stone Fruit Sauce 21

Wild Rice 22

Poultry Recipes...24

Arroz Con Pollo 24

Cabbage Leaves Stuffed With Fruited Brown Rice....................26

Chicken and Mushroom Rice With Soy Sauce and Green Onions 27

Chicken Biryani 29

Chicken Miso Soup With Oyster Mushrooms and Greens.........30

Curried Chicken and Rice 32

Filipino-Style Chicken Adobo 34

Lemon Chicken Soup With Orzo 35

Porcini-Crusted Chicken With Barolo Risotto 36

Seared Chicken With Mushroom-Vegetable Rice.......................38

Southeast Asian Chicken Over Coconut-Pineapple Rice 41

Spicy Chicken and Brown Basmati Rice Lettuce Wraps 43

Spinach Rice With Chicken, Pancetta, and Corn 46

Spinach-Wrapped Chicken Over Brown Rice Pilaf With Soy Dipping Sauce 47

Thai Chicken and Rice Lettuce Wraps With Spicy Mango Relish 50
Turkey and Wild Rice, Rice-Cooker Style 53

Meat 56

Butternut Squash and Sausage Risotto With Fried Sage Leaves 56
Jambalaya 58
Lamb Meatballs With Chimichurri Rice 59
Osso Buco Meatballs With Tomato-Parmesan Risotto 63
Pork and Broccoli Stir-Fry With Noodles 65
Pork Shu Mai Dumplings In Miso Soup 67
Portuguese Sausage and Poached Eggs With Saffron Tomato Sauce 69
Sausage and Peppers With Parmesan Polenta 71
Sweet Sausage and Broccoli Rabe With Farro 73
Veal Meatballs Over Rice With Butternut Squash 75

Seafood 77

Baja Cod With Green Rice 77
Beer-Steamed Shrimp With Lemon Farro 80
Cajun Salmon With Dirty Rice and Fruit Salsa 82
Curried Shrimp With Basmati Rice 87
Garlicky Clam Risotto 88
Halibut With Lemon-Dill Rice 89
Miso Cod Over Black Rice 91
Miso-Glazed Sea Bass Over Quinoa With Vegetables 93
New Orleans–Style Barbecue Shrimp With Cheese and Bacon Grits 94
Paella 96
Parchment-Steamed Sea Bass Veracruz Over Cilantro Quinoa 99
Parsley Pesto Halibut Over White Risotto 100
Scampi With Brown Rice Pilaf 103
Soy-Marinated Salmon With Bok Choy and Coconut Rice 105
Sweet and Pungent Shrimp and Broccoli With Steamed Rice 107

Vegetables and Grains 109

Asparagus and Goat Cheese Frittata 109
Baby Artichoke Farro Pilaf 110
Barley Salad With Pancetta, Corn, and Curry Vinaigrette 112
Beer-Steamed Rice With Black Beans, Corn, and Tomatoes 114
Black Kale and Farro With Garlic–Pine Nut Pesto 115
Black Kale, Winter Squash, and Bulgur Pilaf 117
Broccoli Rabe and Pancetta Bread Pudding 118
Bulgur Risotto With Mixed Mushrooms 120
Curried Cauliflower, Purple Potatoes, and Basmati Rice With Raita 121
Farro Minestrone 124

Garlicky Green Beans With Mixed Vegetable Quinoa Pilaf 125

Grain Salad With Artichokes, Tomatoes, and Fresh Mozzarella 127

Greek Salad With Grains and Lemon-Dill Vinaigrette 128

Italian Chickpea and Pasta Soup 130

Kitchen-Fresh Rice 131

Lemony Quinoa Salad With Tomato and Green Onions 133

Mediterranean Vegetable and Bulgur Stew 134

Nonna's Vegetable Soup..136

Red Beans and Rice..137

Spring Vegetable Risotto 139

Summer Squash Risotto...140

Summertime Grain Salad With Tomatoes, Zucchini, and Basil...........142

Tomato-Parmesan Soup With Ricotta and Spinach Dumplings 143

Tuscan White Bean Soup With Rosemary and Pancetta 145

Umbrian Lentil Stew With Farro 146

Vegetable Biryani...147

Endnote.. **150**

Introduction

The rice cooker is easily one of the most convenient kitchen appliances you can buy today, and has therefore gained, and continues to gain popularity all over the world.

For most of my life, I've cooked rice on a stovetop. The first time I tried the rice cooker, I felt I was a fool for toiling with the gas stove to cook rice for all those years. Once I got a taste for it, there was no going back for me, and I have never cooked without my rice cooker since.

Using a rice cooker is easier, faster, and more energy efficient. It is a versatile little appliance that can be used to cook much more than rice. The final recipe will taste better than that cooked on a stovetop too, if you use the rice cooker right.

Rice cookers have been around for decades now. The first models came without timers, and had to be watched. The rice cookers today, however, have the full grunt of modern technology behind them, and come with high-tech electronics equipped to them. Today, you can guy fuzzy-logic rice cookers, which can be programmed accordingly to the recipe you're cooking. Most of these advanced rice cookers can also be paired to your smartphone, and can be programmed differently for every recipe through the phone itself.

The size and amount of technology you need in your rice cooker will depend on your budget and family size. Feel free to browse amazon for some of the latest models!

A rice cooker uses steam to cook. Steam-cooked food is highly nutritious, and can be insanely delicious too if you know what you're doing. If you're new to the appliance, just follow the recipes in this book, and you will get a hang of how to bring out the full potential of your rice cooker. When you're done with this book, you can use the recipes in this book as a base, and create your own recipes!

If you plan to cook meat using the rice cooker, it is usually a good idea to marinate and brown the meat slightly before throwing into the rice cooker. If you're cooking multiple types on ingredients in the rice cooker simultaneously, know that they will cook in different times, and so you might need to add or remove some of the ingredients during the cook, depending on the recipe. All the recipes in this book will contain detailed directions of when to add or remove an ingredient from the cooker, so follow them closely until you get the hang of the timings yourself.

We will cook all kinds of ingredients and recipes using the rice cooker in this book, but before we get to the recipes, let us discuss the fundamentals of the rice cooker for a bit.

Rice Cooker Fundamentals

How Rice Cookers Work

After you put in rice and water to a rice cooker, the machine brings the water to its boiling point swiftly and then reduces its temperature. Water boils at 212°F/100°C. Once the water has been absorbed and the rice is cooked, the temperature of the rice starts to rise above 212°F/100°C. The machine's thermal sensing device triggers the cooker to turns off or switch to the keep-warm setting. So, when you're cooking food other than rice, you need to watch the timings yourself to make sure all the moisture doesn't get lost.

If you own a fuzzy-logic rice cooker, you will need to reset the cooker to the regular cycle after sautéing. Turn the machine off, and then start again on the regular cycle.

Types of Rice Cookers You Can Buy

Rice cookers come in all sizes and budgets. These are easily available in stores, but amazon will offer a better variety, so I'll advise you to buy one form amazon if you haven't invested in one already. There are three basic types of rice cookers available today, and all three are easily available on amazon.

On/Off Rice Cookers: These are the rice cookers you should buy if you're on a tight budget. These will get the job done just as well as the other ones, but you will need to pay a little attention. The only drawback of these rice cookers is that they will turn off automatically once the rice is done, and you will need to time the steaming process yourself.

On/Off/Warm Rice Cookers: These are slightly costlier than the basic on/off rice cookers due to some added functionality. Once the rice is done, these will switch to "keep warm" mode, so you don't have to serve the recipe immediately.

Fuzzy-Logic Rice Cookers: These are the costliest types of rice cooker you can buy, and the added cost is totally worth it in my opinion. If you have yet to invest in a rice cooker, might as well get the latest tech you can get. These rice cookers have advanced microchips with artificial intelligence programs to make small adjustment in temperature with respect to the contents of the cooker. These rice cookers have a wide array of functions, and you can read all about them when you're about to buy one from a store or on amazon.

In conclusion, I would like to say that if you have the budget, and intend to use the rice cooker extensively, get the most advanced one. It will make your life much easier, and on that you can trust me. As for size, here are the sizes I recommend:

- 1-2 people: Small 3-cup/720-ml Rice Cooker
- 3-5 people: Midsize 5-6-cup/1.2- to 1.4-L Rice Cookers (I own a cooker of this size, and will be using it for all the recipes in this book)

- Large family of 6+: 10-cup/2.4-L Rice Cooker

- Large family of 6+: 10-cup/2.4-L Rice Cooker

Know The Ingredietns

You will do well to add a few of these staples to your pantry, if you haven't already.

BIRYANI PASTE

Biryani is an Indian favorite. Usually, it is rice paired with a meat. This paste can be found in Indian or Asian stores near you, and if you can't, you can always buy them online.

BLACK PEPPER

Fresh black pepper is always more flavorful. Grind your own using a pepper mill, or find a fresh source near you.

BROTH

You will need to use meat or vegetable broth in quite a few recipes in this book. Broth is easily available in stores, and make sure you try all brands and stick with the one you like best!

TOMATOES

Fresh tomatoes are great, but canned tomatoes are convenient. Both will do in a recipe.

DRIED HERBS AND SPICES

These are a staple in any panty. A few of the common ones are: thyme, bay leaves, rosemary, oregano leaves, red pepper flakes, ground cumin, etc. Make sure you always have these on hand, and store them right. You can't go wrong with air-tight containers.

EXTRA-VIRGIN OLIVE OIL

All olive oil isn't EVOO. Read the label carefully before buying.

GARLIC

Buy your garlic fresh, as the flavor is strongest in fresh garlic.

GINGER

Ginger has a strong flavor which uplifts any recipe. Make sure you have some on hand and you store it right.

HOT SAUCE

A good vinegar-based hot sauce really enhances the flavor of a recipe. Make sure you only add as much as you can handle, despite the instructions in a recipe.

PARMIGIANO-REGGIANO CHEESE

A great ingredient to have in your fridge! Goes great with pasta and risotto.

SALT

Sea salt is best. Having a salt grinder in your kitchen helps too.

VEGETABLE OIL

Canola oil and grapeseed oil are my favorites. Always have at least one of these on hand.

A Few Tips For Success With Your Rice Cooker

- If using milk or dairy products in the dish, coat the inside of the rice cooker with nonstick cooking spray or oil for an easy cleanup later.
- Some green herbs are best added at the end of the cooking time, as the don't taste too good steamed.
- Always wash the rice before using. Put the rice in a sieve and run cold water through it.

Basic Rice Recipes

Rice is a staple in most pasts of the world, and in this section, we will look at some basic rice recipes you can make using your rice cooker. Once you get a hang of these, use these as a base to create your own recipes!

Applesauce

Yield: 3 to 4 cups/720 to 960 ml or Servings 6–8

Ingredients:

- ¼ cup/60 ml apple cider or apple juice, plus more if required
- 1 cup/200 g sugar, plus more if required
- 1 Tbsp fresh lemon juice
- 1 tsp ground cinnamon, plus more if required
- 1/8 tsp ground nutmeg, plus more if required
- 4 cups/600 g peeled, cored, and crudely chopped cooking apples

Directions:

1. Mix the apples, apple cider, lemon juice, sugar, cinnamon, and nutmeg in a moderate-sized rice cooker, stirring to combine. Close the lid and cook using regular cycle for half an hour. Stir every ten minutes to ensure

there is enough liquid and the sauce isn't clinging to the bottom. If required, put in slightly more cider.

2. Once the cooking is done, using either an immersion blender or a regular blender, purée the applesauce. Taste for seasoning and adjust by putting in more sugar, cinnamon, or nutmeg. Cool, cover, and place in your fridge for maximum 1 month.

Barley

Yield: 2½ cups/570 g or Servings 4

Ingredients:

- 1 cup/130 g pearled barley
- 2¼ cups/540 ml broth or water

Directions:

1. Put the barley in a sieve and wash under a stable stream of cool water, stirring the grains. Once the water appears to run clear, stop washing and shake the sieve to drain off surplus water.
2. Mix the barley and broth in a moderate-sized rice cooker. Close the lid and cook using regular cycle. Once the cooking is done, allow the barley to carry on steaming for another five minutes on the keep-warm setting or with the machine turned off. If you own a

fuzzy-logic rice cooker, this will be taken care of automatically. Serve hot, or let cool and use in salads.

Brown Rice

Yield: 4 cups/780 g or Servings 4

Ingredients:

- 1 tsp salt
- 2 cups/430 g short-, medium-, or long-grain brown rice
- 3¾ cups/900 ml water or broth

Directions:

1. Put the rice in a sieve and wash under a stable stream of cool water, stirring the grains. Once the water appears to run clear, stop washing and shake the sieve to drain off surplus water.
2. Mix the rice, 3¾ cups/900 ml water, and salt in a moderate-sized rice cooker. Close the lid and cook using regular cycle. Once the cooking is done, let the rice carry on steaming for another ten minutes on the keep-warm setting or with the machine turned off. If you own a fuzzy-logic rice cooker, this will be taken care of automatically. Fluff the rice before you serve.

Bulgur

Yield: 2 cups/460 g or Servings 4

Ingredients:

- 1 cup/215 g medium-grain bulgur
- 1 tsp salt
- 2 cups/480 ml water or broth

Directions:

1. Put the bulgur in a sieve and wash under a stable stream of cool water, stirring the grains. Once the water appears to run clear, stop washing and shake the sieve to drain off surplus water.
2. Mix the bulgur, 2 cups/480 ml water, and salt in a moderate-sized rice cooker. Close the lid and cook using regular cycle. Once the cooking is done, fluff the bulgur and serve hot.

Bulgur Breakfast Porridge

Coat the interior of a moderate-sized rice cooker with nonstick cooking spray. Replace the water with milk and mix with the bulgur and salt in the rice cooker. Close the lid and cook using regular cycle. Set a timer for about twenty minutes. Once the timer finishes, the bulgur must be soft, with some milk left in the cooker. You may need to put in more milk if the bulgur is very sticky. Best served warm.

Dried Beans

Yield: 2½ to 3 cups/570 to 685 g or Servings 4

Ingredients:

- ¼ cup/60 ml extra-virgin olive oil (not necessary)
- 1 cup/200 g dried beans, picked over
- 4 cups/960 ml water
- Salt and freshly ground black pepper (not necessary)

Directions:

1. In a container, cover the beans with 1 in/2.5 cm of water. Allow to soak overnight at room temperature.
2. Drain the beans and mix them with the 4 cups/960 ml water in a moderate-sized rice cooker. Close the lid and cook using regular cycle until the rice cooker turns off by itself; this will take approximately 1½ hours. Drain the beans. Toss with the olive oil and sprinkle with salt and pepper, if you wish, before you serve.

Farro

Yield: 2 cups/330 g or Servings 4

Ingredients:

- 1 cup/200 g farro (pearled or whole grain)
- 1 tsp salt

- 1⅔ cups/405 ml water or broth

Directions:

1. Put the farro in a sieve and wash under a stable stream of cool water, stirring the grains. Once the water appears to run clear, stop washing and shake the sieve to drain off surplus water.
2. Mix the farro, 1⅔ cups/405 ml water, and salt in a moderate-sized rice cooker. Close the lid and cook using regular cycle. Once the cooking is done, allow the farro to carry on steaming for another five minutes on the keep-warm setting or with the machine turned off. If you own a fuzzy-logic rice cooker, this will be taken care of automatically. Fluff the farro before you serve.

FARRO BREAKFAST PORRIDGE

Coat the interior of a moderate-sized rice cooker with nonstick cooking spray. Mix 1 cup/200 g pearled farro, 1⅔ cups/405 ml milk, 1 cup/240 ml water, and 1 tsp salt in the rice cooker. Close the lid and cook using regular cycle. Set a timer for about twenty minutes. Once the timer finishes, the farro must be super soft. If not, cover and cook for an extra five to ten minutes. The porridge must seem like liquidy risotto, with bits of the farro and milky broth. Best served warm.

Grits

Yield: 3 cups/685 g or Servings 4

Ingredients:

- 1 cup/140 g coarse stone-ground grits
- 1 tsp salt
- 2 or 3 dashes hot sauce
- 2 Tbsp unsalted butter
- 2¾ to 3¼ cups/660 to 780 ml water or broth

Directions:

1. Mix the grits, 2¾ cups/660 ml of the water, and the salt in a moderate-sized rice cooker. Close the lid and cook using regular cycle. During the cycle (which may take up to half an hour), stir the grits a few times.
2. If the grits become thick and are starting to stick to the bottom of the pan, mix in a little extra of the water near the end of the cooking time. Once the cooking is done, mix in the butter and hot sauce. Serve hot.

Long-Grain Rice

Yield: 4 cups/780 g or Servings 4

Ingredients:

- ½ tsp salt
- 2 cups/430 g long-grain rice

- 3 cups/720 ml water

Directions:

1. Put the rice in a sieve and wash under a stable stream of cool water, stirring the grains. Once the water appears to run clear, stop washing and shake the sieve to drain off surplus water.
2. Mix the rice, 3 cups/720 ml water, and salt in a moderate-sized rice cooker, cover, and cook using the regular cycle. Once the cooking is done, let the rice carry on steaming for another ten minutes on the keep-warm setting or with the machine turned off. If you own a fuzzy-logic rice cooker, this will be taken care of automatically. Fluff the rice before you serve.

Medium-Grain Rice

Yield: 2 cups/390 g or Servings 4

Ingredients:

- 1 cup/215 g medium-grain rice
- 1 tsp salt
- 3 cups/720 ml water or broth

Directions:

1. Put the rice in a sieve and wash under a stable stream of cool water, stirring the grains. Once the water appears to run clear, stop washing and shake the sieve to drain off surplus water.
2. Mix the rice, 3 cups/720 ml water, and salt in a moderate-sized rice cooker. Close the lid and cook using regular cycle. Once the cooking is done, let the rice carry on steaming for another ten minutes on the keep-warm setting or with the machine turned off. If you own a fuzzy-logic rice cooker, this will be taken care of automatically. Fluff the rice before you serve.

Oatmeal

Yield: 3 cups/685 g or Servings 4

Ingredients:

- ½ tsp salt
- 1 cup/240 ml water
- 1 cup/85 g steel-cut oats
- 1½ cups/360 ml whole milk

Directions:

1. Coat the interior of a moderate-sized rice cooker with nonstick cooking spray. Put in the oats, milk, water, and salt and stir until blended.

2. Close the lid and cook using regular cycle, or to the porridge cycle on fuzzy-logic models. (Check midway through the cooking cycle to ensure it is not running out of liquid and put in more if required.)
3. Once the cooking is done, switch to the warm cycle or switch the machine off and keep covered until you are ready to serve.

Polenta

Yield: 4 cups/915 g or Servings 4

Ingredients:

- 1 cup/140 g Italian coarse-grain cornmeal or polenta
- 1 tsp salt
- 4 cups/960 ml water or vegetable broth

Directions:

1. Coat the interior of a moderate-sized rice cooker with nonstick cooking spray. Put in the polenta, water, and salt and stir until blended. Close the lid and cook using regular cycle.
2. During the cycle, stir once in a while (and put in more water if the polenta is clinging to the pot). Serve hot.

Quinoa

Yield: 2 cups/460 g or Servings 4

Ingredients:

- 1 tsp salt
- 1½ cups/280 g quinoa
- 2¼ cups/540 ml water or broth

Directions:

1. If the quinoa hasn't been prewashed, put it in a fine-mesh sieve and wash with cold water, stirring the quinoa. Once the water appears to run clear and any bits of hull have risen to the top, discard the hulls. (If the quinoa has been prewashed, just give it a quick wash.)
2. Mix the quinoa, 2¼ cups/540 ml water, and salt in a moderate-sized rice cooker. Close the lid and cook using regular cycle. Once the cooking is done, allow the quinoa to carry on steaming for another five minutes on the keep-warm setting or with the machine turned off. If you own a fuzzy-logic rice cooker, this will be taken care of automatically. Serve hot, or let cool and use in salads.

Short-Grain Rice

Yield: 4 cups/780 g or Servings 4

Ingredients:

- 1 tsp salt
- 2 cups/430 g short-grain rice
- 2 cups/480 ml water or broth

Directions:

1. Put the rice in a sieve and wash under a stable stream of cool water, stirring the grains. Once the water appears to run clear, stop washing and shake the sieve to drain off surplus water.

2. Mix the rice, 2 cups/480 ml water, and salt in a moderate-sized rice cooker. Close the lid and cook using regular cycle. Once the cooking is done, let the rice carry on steaming for another ten minutes on the keep-warm setting or with the machine turned off. If you own a fuzzy-logic rice cooker, this will be taken care of automatically. Fluff the rice before you serve.

Stone Fruit Sauce

Yield: 3½ to 4 cups/840 960 ml or Servings 6–8

Ingredients:

- ¼ cup/60 ml peach nectar, plus more if required
- 2 Tbsp fresh lemon juice, plus more if required
- 2 tsp vanilla paste

- 4 cups/600 g peeled, pitted, and crudely chopped stone fruit (peaches, nectarines, plums, or a combination)
- Sugar (not necessary)

Directions:

1. Mix the stone fruit, peach nectar, lemon juice, and vanilla paste in a moderate-sized rice cooker, stirring to combine. Close the lid and cook using regular cycle for half an hour. Stir every ten minutes to ensure there is enough liquid and the sauce isn't clinging to the bottom. If required, put in slightly more peach nectar.
2. Once the cooking is done, using either an immersion blender or a regular blender, purée the sauce. Taste for seasoning and adjust by putting in sugar or more lemon juice. Cool, cover, and place in your fridge for maximum 1 month.

Wild Rice

Yield: 2½ cups/570 g or Servings 4

Ingredients:

- 1 cup/215 g wild rice
- 1 tsp salt
- 2½ cups/600 ml water or broth

Directions:

1. Put the rice in a sieve and wash under a stable stream of cool water, stirring the grains. Once the water appears to run clear, stop washing and shake the sieve to drain off surplus water.

2. Mix the rice, 2½ cups/600 ml water, and salt in a moderate-sized rice cooker. Close the lid and cook using regular cycle. Once the cooking is done, let the rice carry on steaming for another ten minutes on the keep-warm setting or with the machine turned off. If you own a fuzzy-logic rice cooker, this will be taken care of automatically. Fluff the rice before you serve.

Poultry Recipes

Arroz Con Pollo

Ingredients:

- ¼ cup/fifteen g finely chopped fresh cilantro or flat-leaf parsley
- ½ cup/80 g finely chopped red onion
- ½ lb/225 g sweet Italian sausage, casing removed
- ½ tsp ground cumin
- ½ tsp ground turmeric
- 1 bay leaf
- 1 cup/240 ml chicken or vegetable broth
- 1 medium red bell pepper, cored, seeded, and finely chopped
- 1/8 tsp chili powder
- 2 cups/430 g long-grain rice
- 2 garlic cloves, minced
- 2 Tbsp extra-virgin olive oil
- 3 boneless, skinless chicken breast halves (5 to 6 oz/140 to 170 g each), cut into ½-in/12-mm pieces
- One 14½-oz/415-g can chopped tomatoes, with their juice

Directions:

1. Put the rice in a sieve and wash under a stable stream of cool water, stirring the grains. Once the water appears to run clear, stop washing and shake the sieve to drain off surplus water.

2. Set a moderate-sized rice cooker to the regular cycle or to quick cook if using a fuzzy-logic machine. Heat the olive oil, put in the chicken a few pieces at a time, and sauté until white on all sides. Take away the cooked chicken to a plate and continue to sauté until all the chicken is done. Put in the sausage to the pan and sauté until it loses its pink color.

3. Remove all but 1 Tbsp of fat from the pan. Put in the onion, bell pepper, garlic, cumin, chili powder, and turmeric and sauté for about three minutes, or until the vegetables start to become tender. Put the chicken back into the pan and mix in the tomatoes, bay leaf, and rice. Gradually put in the chicken broth.

4. Secure the lid and reset to the regular cycle. At the end of the cooking cycle, stir the rice. Re-cover and carry on steaming for another five minutes on the keep-warm setting or with the machine turned off. If you own a fuzzy-logic rice cooker, this will be taken care of automatically. Move the contents of the rice cooker to a big serving container and serve, decorated with the cilantro.

Cabbage Leaves Stuffed With Fruited Brown Rice

Yield: Servings 4

Ingredients:

- ¼ cup/40 g golden raisins or dried apricots, chopped
- ¼ cup/fifteen g finely chopped fresh flat-leaf parsley
- 1 big egg
- 1 big onion, finely chopped
- 1 lb/455 g ground chicken or turkey
- 1½ cups/295 g cold cooked brown rice
- 2 Tbsp cider vinegar
- 2 Tbsp extra-virgin olive oil
- 2 Tbsp sugar
- 8 big outer leaves of 1 head green cabbage (save the rest for another use)
- One 28-oz/795-g can crushed tomatoes, with their juice
- Salt and freshly ground black pepper

Directions:

1. Position the cabbage leaves on a microwavable plate and cover with a moistened paper towel. Microwave on high for a minute and half a minute, take out of the microwave, and let cool. The cabbage should just be

flexible. If you do not have a microwave, put the cabbage in a big colander and pour boiling water over it.

2. Set a moderate-sized rice cooker to the regular cycle or to quick cook if using a fuzzy-logic machine. Heat the olive oil, put in half the onion, and sauté for two to three minutes, or until aromatic. Mix in the tomatoes, cider vinegar, and sugar. Cover and bring to a simmer.

3. In a big container, mix the chicken, rice, rest of the chopped onion, parsley, raisins, egg, 1 tsp salt, and ½ tsp pepper, stirring thoroughly to mix the ingredients.

4. Place the cabbage leaves on a work surface. Put 2 to 3 Tbsp of the chicken mixture (this will differ depending on the size of the leaf) near the core end of a leaf. Roll up the leaf, folding in the sides as you roll to make a package. Repeat with the rest of the cabbage leaves and chicken mixture. Position the rolls in the sauce in the rice cooker.

5. Secure the lid and reset to the regular cycle. Set a timer for half an hour. Once the timer finishes, ensure that the chicken is thoroughly cooked (an instant-read thermometer inserted into a cabbage leaf should show 165°F/74°C). Sprinkle with salt and pepper, if required. Serve the cabbage rolls warm.

Chicken and Mushroom Rice With Soy Sauce and Green Onions

Ingredients:

- ½ lb/225 g cremini mushrooms, thinly cut
- ½ tsp finely grated peeled fresh ginger
- 1 boneless, skinless chicken breast half (5 to 6 oz/140 to 170 g), finely diced
- 1 garlic clove, minced
- 1 medium carrot, peeled and crudely grated
- 1⅓ cups/285 g long-grain rice
- 2 cups/480 ml chicken or vegetable broth or water
- 2 green onions, white and soft green parts, finely chopped
- 2 Tbsp soy sauce
- 2 Tbsp vegetable oil

Directions:

1. Put the rice in a sieve and wash under a stable stream of cool water, stirring the grains. Once the water appears to run clear, stop washing and shake the sieve to drain off surplus water.

2. Set a moderate-sized rice cooker to the regular cycle or to quick cook if using a fuzzy-logic machine. Put in the vegetable oil, garlic, and ginger and, when the oil starts to sputter, put in the chicken. Sauté until the chicken is white on all sides (it will cook through during the cooking cycle). Put in the mushrooms and carry on cooking until

they start to become tender. Put in the carrot, soy sauce, rice, and chicken broth.

3. Secure the lid and reset to the regular cycle or to mixed cook if using a fuzzy-logic machine. At the end of the cooking cycle, the rice must be soft. Continue steaming for another ten minutes on the keep-warm setting or with the machine turned off. If you own a fuzzy-logic rice cooker, this will be taken care of automatically. Fluff the rice, decorate with the green onions, before you serve.

Chicken Biryani

Ingredients:

- 1 cup/170 g golden raisins
- 1 medium onion, finely chopped
- 1 Tbsp biryani paste (Patak's is a good brand)
- 1 Tbsp vegetable oil
- 1½ cups/315 g basmati rice
- 1½ cups/360 ml plain yogurt
- 2 garlic cloves, minced
- 2 tsp grated peeled fresh ginger
- 2½ cups/600 ml chicken broth
- 4 boneless, skinless chicken breast halves (5 to 6 oz/140 to 170 g each), cut into bite-size pieces

Directions:

1. In a large bowl, mix the yogurt and biryani paste. Put in the chicken and stir until combined. Let the chicken marinate, covered, in your fridge for minimum 2 hours, or maximum 6 hours.
2. Put the rice in a sieve and wash under a stable stream of cool water, stirring the grains. Once the water appears to run clear, stop washing and shake the sieve to drain off surplus water.
3. Set a moderate-sized rice cooker to the regular cycle or to quick cook if using a fuzzy-logic machine. Heat the vegetable oil. Take away the chicken from the marinade using a slotted spoon, saving for later the marinade. Pat the chicken dry using paper towels. In small batches, sauté the chicken until it turns white on all sides and transfer to a plate. Put in the onion, garlic, and ginger to the cooker and sauté for approximately 4 minutes, until the onion starts to turn translucent. Put in the yogurt marinade to the cooker, cover, and bring to its boiling point. Put the chicken back into the cooker and mix in the rice, chicken broth, and raisins.
4. Secure the lid and reset to the regular cycle or to mixed cook if using a fuzzy-logic machine. When the cooker turns off, fluff the rice before you serve.

Chicken Miso Soup With Oyster Mushrooms and Greens

Ingredients:

- ½ cup/115 g white (shiro) miso
- ½ lb/225 g oyster or shiitake mushrooms, finely chopped (remove stems from shiitakes)
- 1 tsp grated peeled fresh ginger
- 1 tsp soy sauce
- 2 boneless, skinless chicken breast halves (5 to 6 oz/140 170 g each), cut into bite-size pieces
- 2 cups/280 g finely chopped greens, such as bok choy, Napa cabbage, or spinach
- 3 green onions, white and soft green parts finely chopped and darker green parts thinly cut for decorate
- 4 cups/960 ml chicken or vegetable broth
- 8 oz/225 g cooked fresh Asian-style thin wheat noodles or cooked thin pasta strands
- Toasted sesame oil for decorate

Directions:

1. Set a moderate-sized rice cooker to the regular cycle or to quick cook if using a fuzzy-logic machine. In a moderate-sized container, pour the soy sauce over the chicken and stir to coat the chicken. Move to the rice cooker and cook until the chicken appears opaque on all sides (it will cook through in the soup). Take away the chicken to a plate. Put in the mushrooms and chopped green onions to the rice cooker and cook for three to

four minutes, until the mushrooms become tender. Put the chicken back into the cooker and put in the ginger. In a big measuring cup, whisk the miso and chicken broth together and pour into the rice cooker. Put in the greens.

2. Secure the lid and reset to the regular cycle. Set a timer for fifteen minutes. Once the timer finishes, open the lid and put in the noodles, stirring to break them up. Cover and cook for an extra two minutes to warm the noodles. Serve the soup decorated with a few drops of sesame oil and the reserved cut green onion tops.

Curried Chicken and Rice

Ingredients:

- ¼ cup/fifteen g finely chopped basil (Thai basil or dark opal basil are especially good)
- ½ cup/120 ml coconut milk
- 1 medium onion, finely chopped
- 1 medium tart apple, peeled, cored, and finely chopped
- 1 to 2 tsp curry powder
- 1 tsp vegetable oil
- 1½ cups/315 g long-grain rice
- 1½ cups/360 ml chicken or vegetable broth
- 2 boneless, skinless chicken breast halves (5 to 6 oz/140 to 170 g each), cut into bite-size pieces

Condiments

- Banana chips
- Chopped peanuts
- Cooked and crumbled bacon
- Finely chopped green onions
- Finely chopped hard-cooked eggs
- Major Grey's chutney
- Shredded coconut
- Sriracha

Directions:

1. Put the rice in a sieve and wash under a stable stream of cool water, stirring the grains. Once the water appears to run clear, stop washing and shake the sieve to drain off surplus water.

2. Set a moderate-sized rice cooker to the regular cycle or to quick cook if using a fuzzy-logic machine. Heat the vegetable oil; put in the onion, apple, and curry powder; and sauté for approximately 3 minutes or until the onion becomes translucent. Put in the chicken and cook until white on all sides (it will cook through during the cooking cycle). Lightly mix in the rice, chicken broth, and coconut milk.

3. Secure the lid and reset to the regular cycle or to mixed cook if using a fuzzy-logic machine. At the end of the

cooking cycle, fluff the rice and drizzle with the basil. Serve with the condiments on the side.

Filipino-Style Chicken Adobo

Ingredients:

- ½ cup/120 ml rice vinegar
- ½ cup/120 ml soy sauce
- ½ tsp freshly ground black pepper
- 1 big onion, finely chopped
- 1 Tbsp grated peeled fresh ginger
- 1 Tbsp vegetable oil
- 2 bay leaves
- 3 cups/585 g cooked short-grain rice for serving
- 3 garlic cloves, minced
- 4 green onions, white and soft green parts, finely chopped
- 6 boneless, skinless chicken thighs

Directions:

1. In a small container, whisk together the soy sauce, rice vinegar, garlic, ginger, onion, black pepper, and bay leaves and save for later.
2. Set a moderate-sized rice cooker to the regular cycle or to quick cook if using a fuzzy-logic machine. Heat the vegetable oil, put in the chicken, and brown on all sides.

Mix in the soy sauce mixture. Secure the lid and reset to the regular cycle. Set a timer for fifteen minutes. Once the timer finishes, turn the chicken, re-cover, and cook for another fifteen minutes. Check the chicken for doneness—it must be soft and thoroughly cooked. Serve the chicken over the rice and decorate with the green onions.

Lemon Chicken Soup With Orzo

Ingredients:

- ½ cup/100 g orzo
- 1 leek, white part only, finely chopped
- 1 Tbsp extra-virgin olive oil
- 2 celery ribs, finely chopped
- 2 cups/280 g finely chopped cooked chicken
- 4 cups/960 ml chicken broth
- Grated zest and juice of 1 lemon, plus thin slices of lemon for garnish
- Salt and freshly ground black pepper (not necessary)
- Sprigs of fresh flat-leaf parsley for decorate

Directions:

1. Set a moderate-sized rice cooker to the regular cycle or to quick cook if using a fuzzy-logic machine. Heat the olive oil and sauté the leek, celery, and lemon zest for

two to three minutes, until the leek starts to become tender. Put in the chicken broth, orzo, and chopped chicken to the pot.

2. Secure the lid and reset to the regular cycle. Set a timer for fifteen minutes. Once the timer finishes, check the orzo; it must be soft. If not, cover and cook for an extra five minutes. Sprinkle with salt and pepper if required. Mix in the lemon juice and serve in soup bowls, decorated with a slice of lemon and a sprig of parsley.

Porcini-Crusted Chicken With Barolo Risotto

Ingredients:

Chicken

- ¼ cup/60 ml extra-virgin olive oil
- ½ cup/100 g dried porcini mushrooms, crushed in the palm of your hand
- ½ tsp freshly ground black pepper
- 1 tsp salt
- 4 boneless, skinless chicken breast halves (5 to 6 oz/140 to 170 g each)

Risotto

- ½ cup/60 g freshly grated Parmigiano-Reggiano

- 1 cup/215 g medium-grain rice, such as Arborio or Carnaroli
- 1 cup/240 ml Barolo wine
- 1 medium shallot, finely chopped
- 1 Tbsp extra-virgin olive oil
- 2 cups/480 ml chicken broth
- 2 tsp finely chopped fresh sage
- 3 Tbsp unsalted butter

Directions:

TO MAKE THE CHICKEN:

1. In a shallow dish, mix the olive oil, salt, and pepper. Place the porcini in a different dish. Immerse the chicken into the oil mixture and then coat with the porcini.
2. Heat a big frying pan using high heat and put in the rest of the oil mixture to the pan. Brown the chicken in batches (it will cook through in the rice cooker) and position in the steamer basket. Set aside.

TO MAKE THE RISOTTO:

1. Put the rice in a sieve and wash under a stable stream of cool water, stirring the grains. Once the water appears to run clear, stop washing and shake the sieve to drain off surplus water.
2. Set a moderate-sized rice cooker to the regular cycle or to quick cook if using a fuzzy-logic machine. Heat the

olive oil and 1 Tbsp of the butter until the butter melts. Put in the shallot and sage and sauté for approximately 3 minutes or until the shallot starts to become tender. Put in the Barolo and bring to its boiling point. Mix in the rice and coat with the Barolo mixture. Put in the chicken broth. Position the steamer basket over the rice cooker.

3. Secure the lid and reset to the regular cycle or to the porridge cycle on a fuzzy-logic machine. Set a timer for about twenty minutes. Once the timer finishes, test the chicken for doneness (it should read 165°F/74°C on an instant-read thermometer). Cut the chicken into ½-in/12-mm strips. Mix the rest of the 2 Tbsp butter and the Parmigiano into the risotto. Move the risotto to a serving platter, put the chicken over the risotto, before you serve.

Seared Chicken With Mushroom-Vegetable Rice

Ingredients:

Chicken

- ¼ cup/50 g sugar
- ¼ cup/60 ml soy sauce
- ½ cup/120 ml mirin (Japanese sweet rice wine)
- 1 Tbsp toasted sesame oil

- 1 tsp grated peeled fresh ginger
- 2 garlic cloves, minced
- 2 Tbsp ketchup
- 4 boneless, skinless chicken breast halves (5 to 6 oz/140 to 170 g each)

Rice

- ½ lb/225 g shiitake mushrooms, stemmed and finely chopped
- 1 garlic clove, minced
- 1 medium carrot, peeled and crudely grated
- 1 medium zucchini, crudely grated
- 1 Tbsp toasted sesame seeds
- 1 Tbsp vegetable oil
- 2 cups/430 g long-grain rice
- 2 green onions, white and soft green parts, finely chopped
- 2¾ cups/660 ml chicken or vegetable broth

Directions:

TO MAKE THE CHICKEN:

1. Put the chicken breasts in a big zipper-top plastic bag. In a small container, whisk together the soy sauce, mirin, sugar, ketchup, garlic, ginger, and sesame oil.

2. Pour the mixture over the chicken, seal the bag, and marinate the chicken in your fridge for minimum 2 hours, or maximum 8 hours. When ready to cook, drain the marinade into a small deep cooking pan and boil gently for five minutes. Reduce the heat and simmer until syrupy. Set aside for serving.

3. Pat the chicken dry using paper towels. Heat a nonstick grill pan or frying pan on moderate to high heat and sear the chicken breasts on both sides, so that they have nice color. Position in the steamer basket and save for later.

TO MAKE THE RICE:

1. Put the rice in a sieve and wash under a stable stream of cool water, stirring the grains. Once the water appears to run clear, stop washing and shake the sieve to drain off surplus water.

2. Set a moderate-sized rice cooker to the regular cycle or to quick cook if using a fuzzy-logic machine. Heat the vegetable oil, put in the garlic and mushrooms, and sauté for approximately 3 minutes, or until the mushroom liquid starts to evaporate. Put in the zucchini and carrot and sauté for another one minute. Mix in the rice and progressively put in the chicken broth. Position the steamer basket over the rice.

3. Secure the lid and reset to the regular cycle. While the rice and chicken are cooking, reheat the sauce so that it is warm when the rice is finished. Once the cycle ends,

check the chicken for doneness; it should show 165°F/74°C on an instant-read thermometer. Mix the green onions into the rice and position on a big serving platter. Chop the chicken on the diagonal into fine strips and position over the rice. Sprinkle some of the sauce over the chicken, drizzle with the sesame seeds, before you serve.

Southeast Asian Chicken Over Coconut-Pineapple Rice

Ingredients:

Chicken

- ¼ cup/60 ml coconut milk
- ¼ cup/60 ml fish sauce
- ¼ tsp Sriracha
- 1 garlic clove, minced
- 1 tsp grated peeled fresh ginger
- 2 Tbsp tightly packed light brown sugar
- 4 boneless, skinless chicken breast halves (5 to 6 oz/140 to 170 g each)

Rice

- 1 cup/240 ml coconut milk

- 1 cup/240 ml pineapple juice
- 1 cup/240 ml water
- 1½ cups/230 g chopped fresh pineapple
- 2 cups/430 g long-grain rice
- 2 Tbsp finely chopped fresh mint
- 3 green onions, white and soft green parts, finely chopped
- Chopped pineapple for decorate

Directions:

TO MAKE THE CHICKEN:

1. Put the chicken breasts in a big zipper-top plastic bag. In a small container, whisk together the garlic, ginger, Sriracha, fish sauce, brown sugar, and coconut milk.
2. Pour the mixture over the chicken in the bag and place in your fridge for minimum 2 hours, or maximum 8 hours. Drain the marinade and pat the chicken dry using paper towels. Heat a big frying pan on moderate to high heat and sear the chicken on both sides to brown. Position the chicken in the steamer basket of the rice cooker and save for later.

TO MAKE THE RICE:

1. Put the rice in a sieve and wash under a stable stream of cool water, stirring the grains. Once the water appears

to run clear, stop washing and shake the sieve to drain off surplus water.

2. Move to a moderate-sized rice cooker and put in the 1 cup/240 ml water, coconut milk, pineapple juice, and fresh pineapple, stirring well. Position the steamer basket on top of the rice.

3. Secure the lid and set to the regular cycle or to quick cook if using a fuzzy-logic machine. Once the cycle ends, check to ensure the chicken is thoroughly cooked. (It should show 165°F/74°C on an instant-read thermometer.) Re-cover and carry on steaming for another five minutes on the keep-warm setting or with the machine turned off. If you own a fuzzy-logic rice cooker, this will be taken care of automatically. Chop the chicken on the diagonal into strips ½ in/12 mm thick. Fluff the rice, position on a serving platter, and position the chicken over the rice. Drizzle with the green onions and mint and position any additional pineapple around the rim of the platter to serve.

Spicy Chicken and Brown Basmati Rice Lettuce Wraps

Ingredients:

- ¼ cup/60 ml soy sauce
- ½ cup/110 g brown basmati rice

- ¾ cup/180 ml chicken or vegetable broth
- 1 head iceberg or butterhead lettuce, leaves separated
- 1 Tbsp hoisin sauce
- 1 Tbsp toasted sesame oil
- 1 tsp grated peeled fresh ginger
- 2 boneless, skinless chicken breast halves (5 to 6 oz/140 to 170 g each), cut into ½-in/12-mm pieces
- 2 garlic cloves, minced
- 2 green onions, white and soft green parts, finely chopped
- 2 Tbsp mirin (Japanese sweet rice wine)
- 2 Tbsp vegetable oil
- 3 or 4 dashes Sriracha (not necessary)
- One 8-oz/225-g can water chestnuts, drained and finely chopped
- Sweet and Spicy Soy Sauce (recipe follows) for serving (not necessary)

Directions:

1. In a moderate-sized container, mix the chicken, soy sauce, mirin, hoisin, and Sriracha (if using), stirring to coat the chicken. Set aside.
2. Put the rice in a sieve and wash under a stable stream of cool water, stirring the grains. Once the water appears to run clear, stop washing and shake the sieve to drain off surplus water.

3. Set a moderate-sized rice cooker to the regular cycle or to quick cook if using a fuzzy-logic machine. Heat the vegetable oil, put in the garlic and ginger, and sauté for a minute, or until aromatic. Put in the chicken and marinade and cook, stirring, until the chicken turns white on all sides (it will cook through with the rice). Put in the water chestnuts and rice, stirring to coat the rice. Mix in the chicken broth.

4. Secure the lid and reset to the regular cycle, or to mixed cook if using a fuzzy-logic machine. Once the rice is done cooking, mix in the sesame oil and green onions. Move to a serving container. Pass the lettuce leaves separately for each diner to wrap their own, together with the sweet and spicy soy sauce, if you wish.

SWEET AND SPICY SOY SAUCE

Yield: ¼ CUP/60 ML

Ingredients:

- 1 garlic clove, minced
- 1 green onion, white and soft green parts, finely chopped
- 1 Tbsp mirin (Japanese sweet rice wine)
- 1 tsp sugar
- 1 tsp toasted sesame oil
- 2 Tbsp soy sauce, plus more if required
- 3 dashes Sriracha, plus more if required

Directions:

1. In a small container, whisk together the soy sauce, sugar, mirin, Sriracha, garlic, sesame oil, and green onion.
2. Taste for seasoning and put in more Sriracha or soy sauce as required. Store in your fridge for maximum four days.

Spinach Rice With Chicken, Pancetta, and Corn

Yield: Servings 4–6

Ingredients:

- ½ cup/80 g finely chopped sweet yellow onion, such as Vidalia
- 1 garlic clove, minced
- 2 boneless, skinless chicken breast halves (5 to 6 oz/140 to 170 g each), cut into bite-size pieces
- 2 cups/280 g packed baby spinach, crudely chopped
- 2 cups/340 g corn kernels, cut fresh from the cob, or frozen kernels (do not defrost)
- 2 cups/430 g brown basmati or other long-grain rice
- 2 Tbsp extra-virgin olive oil
- 3 cups/720 ml chicken or vegetable broth
- One ½-in-/12-mm-thick slice pancetta, finely diced

Directions:

1. Put the rice in a sieve and wash under a stable stream of cool water, stirring the grains. Once the water appears to run clear, stop washing and shake the sieve to drain off surplus water.
2. Set a moderate-sized rice cooker to the regular cycle or to quick cook if using a fuzzy-logic machine. Heat the olive oil, put in the pancetta, and sauté until it becomes crunchy. Put in the garlic and onion and sauté for another three minutes, or until the onion becomes tender. Put in the chicken and sauté until the chicken is white on all sides. Put in the corn and rice and stir until blended. Gradually put in the chicken broth.
3. Secure the lid and reset to the regular cycle. Once the cycle ends, mix in the spinach. Re-cover and carry on steaming for another five minutes on the keep-warm setting or with the machine turned off. If you own a fuzzy-logic rice cooker, this will be taken care of automatically. Serve warm.

Spinach-Wrapped Chicken Over Brown Rice Pilaf With Soy Dipping Sauce

Ingredients:

Chicken

- ¼ cup/60 ml mirin (Japanese sweet rice wine)
- ½ cup/120 ml soy sauce
- 1 lb/455 g big spinach leaves, tough stems removed
- 1 tsp grated peeled fresh ginger
- 2 garlic cloves, minced
- 2 Tbsp sugar
- 4 boneless, skinless chicken breast halves (5 to 6 oz/140 to 170 g each)

Rice and Edamame

- 1 cup/170 g frozen shelled edamame, thawed
- 1 medium onion, finely chopped
- 1 Tbsp vegetable oil
- 2 cups/430 g brown rice
- 3¾ cups/900 ml chicken or vegetable broth

Dipping Sauce

- ¼ cup/50 g sugar
- ¾ cup/180 ml soy sauce
- 1 garlic clove, minced
- 1 Tbsp rice vinegar
- 1 tsp grated peeled fresh ginger
- 2 green onions, white and soft green parts, thinly cut on the diagonal
- 2 Tbsp toasted sesame oil

- 2 Tbsp toasted sesame seeds

Directions:

TO MAKE THE CHICKEN:

1. Put the chicken into a big zipper-top plastic bag. In a small container, whisk together the soy sauce, mirin, sugar, garlic, and ginger. Pour the marinade over the chicken, seal the bag, and marinate for minimum 2 hours, or maximum 8 hours, in your fridge.
2. Position the spinach leaves on a microwavable plate and cover with a moistened paper towel. Microwave on high for twenty seconds, just to tenderize the spinach. If you do not have a microwave, put the spinach in a colander and pour boiling water over it. Drain the marinade and pat the chicken dry using paper towels. Cover each chicken breast in several spinach leaves, position in the steamer basket of the rice cooker, and save for later.

TO MAKE THE RICE AND EDAMAME:

1. Put the rice in a sieve and wash under a stable stream of cool water, stirring the grains. Once the water appears to run clear, stop washing and shake the sieve to drain off surplus water.
2. Set a moderate-sized rice cooker to the regular cycle or to quick cook if using a fuzzy-logic machine. Heat the vegetable oil, put in the onion, and sauté for a couple of

minutes, or until it starts to become tender. Put in the rice and cook for an extra two minutes, to toast the grains. Gradually mix in the chicken broth. Position the steamer basket over the rice.

3. Secure the lid and reset to the regular cycle or to the brown-rice cycle on a fuzzy-logic machine. Once the cycle ends, check the chicken for doneness; it should show 165°F/74°C on an instant-read thermometer. Mix the rice and put in the edamame. Re-cover and carry on steaming for another five minutes on the keep-warm setting or with the machine turned off. If you own a fuzzy-logic rice cooker, this will be taken care of automatically.

MEANWHILE, MAKE THE DIPPING SAUCE:

1. In a small container, mix the soy sauce, sesame oil, rice vinegar, ginger, garlic, sugar, and green onions, stirring to combine. Mix in the sesame seeds just before you serve.
2. Take away the chicken from the steamer basket. Position the rice on a serving platter and top with the chicken. Sprinkle some of the dipping sauce over the chicken and serve the rest on the side.

Thai Chicken and Rice Lettuce Wraps With Spicy Mango Relish

Yield: Servings 4–6

Ingredients:

- ½ cup/110 g jasmine rice
- ½ cup/25 g bean sprouts
- ½ cup/30 g chopped fresh cilantro
- ½ cup/30 g firmly packed basil leaves, finely chopped, plus additional whole or cut leaves
- ½ cup/80 g finely diced shallots
- 1 butterhead lettuce, leaves separated
- 1 Tbsp soy sauce
- 1 Tbsp sugar
- 1 to 2 green or red Thai chiles, stemmed and finely chopped
- 1 tsp rice vinegar
- 1½ cups/360 ml chicken or vegetable broth
- 1½ lb/680 g boneless, skinless chicken breast, cut into little pieces, or 1½ lb/680 g ground chicken or turkey
- 2 Tbsp fish sauce
- 2 Tbsp vegetable oil
- 3 garlic cloves, minced
- 3 green onions, white and soft green parts, finely chopped
- Spicy Mango Relish for serving (not necessary)

Directions:

1. Put the rice in a sieve and wash under a stable stream of cool water, stirring the grains. Once the water appears to run clear, stop washing and shake the sieve to drain off surplus water.

2. Set a moderate-sized rice cooker to the regular cycle or to quick cook if using a fuzzy-logic machine. Heat the vegetable oil, put in the garlic and shallots, and sauté for a minute, or until aromatic. Put in the chiles and continue sautéing for two to three minutes, until the chiles start to become tender. Put in the chicken and sauté until it is no longer pink in color, breaking up the clumps if ground. If there is surplus water in the pan, drain a small amount of it. Put in the fish sauce, soy sauce, rice vinegar, and sugar. Stir to combine. Mix the rice into the chicken mixture and pour in the chicken broth.

3. Secure the lid and reset to the regular cycle. Once the cycle ends, stir the chicken and rice mixture. Re-cover and carry on steaming for another ten minutes on the keep-warm setting or with the machine turned off. If you own a fuzzy-logic rice cooker, this will be taken care of automatically. Mound the chicken and rice in a serving container. Place the lettuce, basil, cilantro, green onions, and bean sprouts in different bowls and allow each diner to make his/her own tender taco. Serve with the mango relish, if you wish.

SPICY MANGO RELISH

Yield: ½ CUP/90 G

Ingredients:

- 1 big mango, peeled and finely chopped
- 1 Tbsp fresh lime juice
- 1 Tbsp soy sauce
- 1 tsp finely chopped red Thai chile
- 1 tsp finely grated peeled fresh ginger
- 2 garlic cloves, minced
- 2 Tbsp finely chopped red onion
- 2 tsp sugar
- 3 Tbsp fish sauce

Directions:

1. In a moderate-sized mixing container, mix the chile, red onion, garlic, ginger, fish sauce, soy sauce, lime juice, and sugar, whisking to dissolve the sugar.
2. Put in the mango and toss until mixed. Cover and place in your fridge for maximum 3 days.

Turkey and Wild Rice, Rice-Cooker Style

Ingredients:

- ¼ cup/25 g toasted cut almonds

- ½ cup/80 g finely chopped red onion
- ½ cup/85 g dried cranberries, chopped if large
- 1 cup/215 g wild rice
- 1 medium carrot, peeled and finely chopped
- 1 Tbsp extra-virgin olive oil
- 1 Tbsp unsalted butter
- 1 tsp dried thyme
- 1½ cups/210 g cooked turkey or chicken, finely chopped
- 2 celery ribs, finely chopped
- 2 Tbsp finely chopped fresh flat-leaf parsley
- 2½ cups/600 ml chicken or vegetable broth
- Salt and freshly ground black pepper

Directions:

1. Put the wild rice in a sieve and wash under a stable stream of cool water, stirring the grains. Once the water appears to run clear, stop washing and shake the sieve to drain off surplus water.
2. Set a moderate-sized rice cooker to the regular cycle or to quick cook if using a fuzzy-logic machine. Melt the butter with the olive oil. Put in the onion, celery, carrot, and thyme and sauté for about three minutes, or until the onion starts to become tender. Put in the rice, turkey, and cranberries, stirring to combine. Slowly mix in the chicken broth.

3. Secure the lid and reset to the regular cycle. Set a timer for about twenty-five minutes. Once the timer finishes, check the rice; there should still be a small amount of liquid in the pan. The rice should have split open, and it must be soft. Sprinkle with salt and pepper and move to a big serving container. Decorate using the almonds and chopped parsley before you serve.

Meat

Butternut Squash and Sausage Risotto With Fried Sage Leaves

Ingredients:

Fried Sage Leaves

- ¼ cup/60 ml extra-virgin olive oil
- 6 sage leaves

Risotto

- ¼ cup/60 ml white wine (Sauvignon Blanc or Pinot Grigio)
- ⅓ cup/45 g freshly grated Parmigiano-Reggiano cheese
- ½ lb/225 g sweet Italian sausage, removed from its casing
- 1 cup/215 g medium-grain rice, such as Arborio or Carnaroli
- 1 medium shallot, finely chopped
- 1½ cups/340 g finely chopped peeled and seeded butternut squash
- 2 Tbsp unsalted butter

- 2½ cups/500 ml chicken or vegetable broth

Directions:

TO MAKE THE FRIED SAGE LEAVES:

1. Set a moderate-sized rice cooker to the regular cycle or to quick cook if using a fuzzy-logic machine. Heat the olive oil, put in the sage leaves, and fry until they are crunchy.
2. Remove to paper towels and drain. Move the oil from the rice cooker to a measuring cup and save for later.

TO MAKE THE RISOTTO:

1. Put the rice in a sieve and wash under a stable stream of cool water, stirring the grains. Once the water appears to run clear, stop washing and shake the sieve to drain off surplus water.
2. Sauté the sausage in the rice cooker until it loses its pink color, breaking up any bigger pieces. Put in the shallot and butternut squash and cook for approximately 3 minutes, or until the shallot starts to become tender. Put in the wine and chicken broth and bring to its boiling point. Put in the rice and stir to coat the grains.
3. Secure the lid and reset to the regular cycle. At the end of the cooking cycle, check the risotto; there should still be a small amount of liquid in the pan, and the rice must be firm to the bite (still firm to the bite). Mix in the

butter and half of the Parmigiano. Serve the risotto in shallow bowls, decorated with a sprinkle of the sage oil and a leaf of sage, and pass the rest of the Parmigiano on the side.

Jambalaya

Ingredients:

- ¼ tsp dried oregano
- ½ lb/225 g andouille or another smoked sausage
- ½ lb/225 g big shrimp, peeled, deveined, and chopped
- ½ tsp dried thyme
- ½ tsp sweet paprika
- 1 medium onion, finely chopped
- 1 medium red bell pepper, cored, seeded, and finely chopped
- 1 Tbsp tomato paste
- 1/8 tsp cayenne pepper
- 1½ cups/315 g long-grain rice
- 2 celery ribs, finely chopped
- 2 cups/480 ml chicken or vegetable broth
- 2 garlic cloves, minced
- 2 green onions, white and soft green parts, finely chopped
- Assorted hot sauces for serving

Directions:

1. Put the rice in a sieve and wash under a stable stream of cool water, stirring the grains. Once the water appears to run clear, stop washing and shake the sieve to drain off surplus water.
2. Set a moderate-sized rice cooker to the regular cycle or to quick cook if using a fuzzy-logic machine. Sauté the sausage until it renders some fat. Put in the onion, celery, bell pepper, garlic, paprika, thyme, oregano, and cayenne. Sauté for three to four minutes, or until the onion is translucent. Put in the tomato paste and stir to combine. Mix in the rice and chicken broth.
3. Secure the lid and reset to the regular cycle. At the end of the cooking cycle, mix in the shrimp and close the lid. Set a timer for about ten minutes. Once the timer finishes, the shrimp must be pink and thoroughly cooked. Fluff the rice and decorate the jambalaya with the green onions. Pass the hot sauces on the side at the time of serving.

Lamb Meatballs With Chimichurri Rice

Ingredients:

Chimichurri

- 1 Tbsp finely chopped fresh oregano
- 1½ cups/90 g packed fresh flat-leaf parsley
- 2 Tbsp capers packed in brine, drained
- 2 Tbsp extra-virgin olive oil
- 2 Tbsp red wine vinegar
- 4 garlic cloves, minced
- Pinch of red pepper flakes

Meatballs

- ½ cup/80 g finely chopped red onion
- ½ tsp freshly ground black pepper
- 1 big egg, beaten
- 1 lb/455 g ground lamb
- 1½ tsp salt
- 2 garlic cloves, minced
- 2 Tbsp finely chopped fresh mint
- Extra-virgin olive oil for frying
- Grated zest of 1 lemon

Rice

- 2 cups/430 g long-grain rice
- 3 cups/720 ml chicken or vegetable broth

Directions:

TO MAKE THE CHIMICHURRI:

1. In a food processor or blender, process the parsley, garlic, red pepper flakes, oregano, capers, red wine vinegar, and olive oil until you have a smooth sauce. Set aside. (It will keep in your fridge for maximum four days.)

TO MAKE THE MEATBALLS:

1. In a big mixing container, mix together the lamb, garlic, lemon zest, mint, onion, salt, pepper, and egg until well blended. Using a portion scoop, shape the mixture into 1-in/2.5-cm balls. In a big frying pan, heat ½ in/12 mm olive oil and brown the meatballs in batches.
2. Drain over paper towels. Position the meatballs in a steamer basket—you may have to stack them—and save for later. (At this point, you can cool the meatballs, place in your fridge them for maximum 8 hours, and then proceed with the recipe.)

TO MAKE THE RICE:

1. Put the rice in a sieve and wash under a stable stream of cool water, stirring the grains. Once the water appears to run clear, stop washing and shake the sieve to drain off surplus water.
2. In a moderate-sized rice cooker, mix the rice and chicken broth, stirring until mixed. Position the steamer basket over the rice.

3. Secure the lid and set to the regular cycle. When the rice is done, remove the steamer basket. Put in half of the chimichurri to the rice and stir to combine. Move the rice to a platter and position the meatballs over the rice, drizzling with a small amount of the rest of the chimichurri before you serve.

Osso Buco Meatballs With Tomato-Parmesan Risotto

Ingredients:

Meatballs

- 1 big egg, beaten
- 1 cup/115 g dry bread crumbs
- 1 cup/55 g torn fresh bread
- 1 garlic clove, minced
- 1 lb/455 g ground veal
- 1 tsp grated lemon zest
- 1 tsp grated orange zest
- 1/8 tsp saffron threads, crushed in the palm of your hand
- 2 tsp minced flat-leaf parsley
- 3 Tbsp milk
- Extra-virgin olive oil for frying

Risotto

- ¼ cup/25 g chopped rinds from Parmigiano-Reggiano (not necessary), plus ⅓ cup/45 g freshly grated Parmigiano-Reggiano
- ¼ cup/60 ml dry white wine or dry vermouth
- 1 medium shallot, finely chopped

- 1 Tbsp extra-virgin olive oil
- 1½ cups/230 g cherry or pear tomatoes, chopped
- 2 cups/430 g medium-grain rice, such as Arborio or Carnaroli
- 2 fresh sage leaves, finely chopped
- 2¾ cups/660 ml chicken or vegetable broth
- 4 Tbsp/55 g unsalted butter
- Basil for garnish (not necessary)

Directions:

TO MAKE THE MEATBALLS:

1. Place the bread in a big mixing container and pour the milk over the bread. Let stand for five minutes, or until the milk is absorbed. Put in the veal, lemon zest, orange zest, parsley, saffron, garlic, and egg and stir until the mixture is meticulously blended. Spread out the dry bread crumbs in a uniform layer on a plate. Using a portion scoop, shape the mixture into 1-in/2.5-cm balls and then roll in the bread crumbs until coated.
2. In a big frying pan, heat ½ in/12 mm of olive oil and fry the meatballs in batches, turning regularly to give them a nice crust. Drain over paper towels. Position the meatballs in the steamer basket—you may have to stack them—and save for later. (At this point, you can cool the meatballs, place in your fridge them for maximum 8 hours, and then proceed with the recipe.)

TO MAKE THE RISOTTO:

1. Put the rice in a sieve and wash under a stable stream of cool water, stirring the grains. Once the water appears to run clear, stop washing and shake the sieve to drain off surplus water.
2. Set a moderate-sized rice cooker to the regular cycle or to quick cook if using a fuzzy-logic machine. Melt the butter with the olive oil, put in the shallot and sage, and sauté for two to three minutes, or until the shallot is translucent. Put in the rice and tomatoes and sauté for another three minutes, until the tomatoes start to become tender. Put in the wine, chicken broth, and Parmigiano rinds (if using).
3. Position the steamer basket over the rice. Secure the lid and reset to the regular cycle. Set a timer for about twenty minutes. Once the timer finishes, check the risotto; it should still have a small amount of liquid in the pan, and the rice must be firm to the bite (still firm to the bite). Take away the steamer basket, stir the grated Parmigiano into the risotto, and move to a platter. Position the meatballs on top of the risotto and decorate with basil (if using) before you serve.

Pork and Broccoli Stir-Fry With Noodles

Ingredients:

- ¼ cup/60 ml tamari or soy sauce
- ½ cup/120 ml chicken or vegetable broth
- ½ cup/55 g chopped roasted salted cashews
- ½ lb/225 g pork tenderloin, cut into ½-in/12-mm strips
- ½ tsp chili-garlic sauce (not necessary)
- 1 cup/160 g broccoli florets
- 1 garlic clove, minced
- 1 lb/455 g cooked fresh Asian-style thin wheat noodles or cooked thin pasta strands
- 1 medium onion, thinly cut
- 1 Tbsp ketchup
- 1 tsp grated peeled fresh ginger
- 2 green onions, white and soft green parts, finely chopped
- 2 Tbsp rice vinegar
- 2 Tbsp vegetable oil
- 2 tsp cornstarch

Directions:

1. Set a moderate-sized rice cooker to the regular cycle or to quick cook if using a fuzzy-logic machine. Heat the vegetable oil, put in the garlic and ginger, and sauté for half a minute, or until aromatic. Put in the pork and stir-fry until the pork is white on all sides (it may not be thoroughly cooked now). Take away the pork to a plate,

put in the onion and broccoli to the pan, and stir-fry until they start to tenderize, approximately 3 minutes.

2. In a small container, mix together the tamari, ketchup, rice vinegar, chili-garlic sauce (if using), cornstarch, and chicken broth until the cornstarch is dissolved. Put the pork back into the rice cooker and pour in the sauce, stirring to blend. Position the noodles in the steamer basket and set over the pork.

3. Secure the lid and reset to the regular cycle. Set a timer for about ten minutes. Once the timer finishes, move the noodles to a platter, stir the pork mixture, and position over the noodles. Drizzle with the green onions and cashews before you serve.

Pork Shu Mai Dumplings In Miso Soup

Ingredients:

Dumplings

- ½ cup/85 g finely chopped water chestnuts
- 1 lb/455 g ground pork
- 1 Tbsp cornstarch
- 1 Tbsp mirin (Japanese sweet rice wine)
- 1 Tbsp toasted sesame oil
- 1 tsp grated peeled fresh ginger
- 2 garlic cloves, minced

- 2 green onions, white and soft green parts, finely chopped
- 2 Tbsp tamari or soy sauce
- One 10-oz/280-g package wonton wrappers

Soup

1. 2 Tbsp vegetable oil
2. 1 tsp grated peeled fresh ginger
3. ½ cup/115 g white (shiro) miso
4. 4 cups/960 ml chicken or vegetable broth
5. 2 cups/280 g finely chopped greens, such as bok choy, Napa cabbage, or spinach
6. 3 green onions; white and soft green parts, finely chopped; darker green parts, thinly cut for decoration

Directions:

TO MAKE THE DUMPLINGS:

1. In a moderate-sized container, mix the pork, tamari, sesame oil, mirin, ginger, garlic, water chestnuts, green onions, and cornstarch, stirring until mixed. Using a small portion scoop or a teaspoon, make the mixture into approximately twenty-four balls and place each one in the middle of a wonton wrapper.
2. Bring up the sides of the wrapper around the pork, twisting them closed to make a small purse out of the dough and securing the edges with a small amount of

water. Set the finished dumplings on a baking sheet coated with parchment paper. (If you are not using them instantly, cover and place in your fridge for maximum 8 hours.)

TO MAKE THE SOUP:

1. Set a moderate-sized rice cooker to the regular cycle or to quick cook if using a fuzzy-logic machine. Heat the vegetable oil, put in the ginger, and sauté for a minute, or until it is aromatic. Put in the miso, chicken broth, and greens. Position the dumplings in two steamer baskets and place in the rice cooker.

2. Secure the lid and reset to the regular cycle. Set a timer for about twenty minutes. Once the timer finishes, check to ensure the dumplings are thoroughly cooked (they should show 160°F/71°C on an instant-read thermometer). Take away the dumplings from the steamer baskets and put in a soup tureen. Put in the green onions to the soup and pour over the dumplings. Serve instantly.

Portuguese Sausage and Poached Eggs With Saffron Tomato Sauce

Ingredients:

- ¼ cup/fifteen g finely chopped fresh flat-leaf parsley

- ½ cup/120 ml chicken broth
- ½ lb/225 g linguiça or another smoked sausage, cut into ½-in/12-mm rounds
- 1 big onion, finely chopped
- 1 cup/100 g frozen petite peas, defrosted
- 1 garlic clove, minced
- 1 red bell pepper, cored, seeded, and finely chopped
- 1 tsp saffron threads, crushed in the palm of your hand
- 4 big eggs
- Crusty bread for serving
- One 14½- to fifteen-oz/415- to 430-g can chopped tomatoes, with their juice
- Salt and freshly ground black pepper

Directions:

1. Set a moderate-sized rice cooker to the regular cycle or to quick cook if using a fuzzy-logic machine. Sauté the sausage, onion, and garlic for about three minutes, or until the sausage has rendered some fat.
2. Remove all but 2 Tbsp of fat from the pan and put in the bell pepper and saffron, stirring to coat the vegetables and meat with the saffron. Put in the tomatoes and chicken broth and cover the rice cooker. Reset to the regular cycle and set a timer for about twenty minutes. Once the timer finishes, flavor the sauce with salt and pepper. Crack the eggs into a measuring cup. Put in the

peas to the sauce, slide the eggs over the sauce, and drizzle with more salt and pepper, if you wish.

3. Secure the lid and cook for five minutes, until the eggs are set. (Depending on your rice cooker, this could take a small amount longer.) Cautiously remove the eggs from the rice cooker with some of the sauce, and plate them. Decorate using the chopped parsley and serve with crusty bread to mop up the delicious sauce.

Sausage and Peppers With Parmesan Polenta

Ingredients:

Sausage and Peppers

- ¼ cup/fifteen g finely chopped fresh basil
- ¼ cup/fifteen g finely chopped fresh flat-leaf parsley
- ½ tsp dried oregano
- 1 big orange bell pepper, cored, seeded, and thinly cut
- 1 big red bell pepper, cored, seeded, and thinly cut
- 1 big sweet yellow onion, such as Vidalia, thinly cut
- 1 big yellow bell pepper, cored, seeded, and thinly cut
- 1½ lb/680 g sweet Italian sausage, or a mix of sweet and spicy
- 2 Tbsp aged balsamic vinegar

- 2 Tbsp extra-virgin olive oil
- One 14½-oz/415-g can crushed tomatoes, with their juice
- Salt and freshly ground black pepper

Polenta

- ½ cup/60 g freshly grated Parmigiano-Reggiano cheese
- 1 cup/140 g Italian coarse-grain polenta
- 1 tsp salt
- 2 cups/480 ml water or vegetable or chicken broth
- 2 cups/480 ml whole milk
- 3 Tbsp unsalted butter

Directions:

TO MAKE THE SAUSAGE AND PEPPERS:

1. In a big frying pan, heat the olive oil on moderate to high heat. Sear the sausage, ensuring that it is browned on all sides. Remove from the frying pan and save for later. Put in the onion and bell peppers to the frying pan and sauté for five to seven minutes, until the vegetables start to become tender.
2. Put in the tomatoes, oregano, and balsamic vinegar and bring to its boiling point. Return the sausages to the pan and simmer for about twenty minutes, until the sauce is reduced and the sausages are thoroughly cooked. Taste

for seasoning and adjust with salt and pepper. Mix in the basil and parsley and keep warm.

TO MAKE THE POLENTA:

1. While the sausages are cooking, coat the inside of a moderate-sized rice cooker with nonstick cooking spray. Mix the water, milk, polenta, and salt in the rice cooker. Close the lid and cook using regular cycle. During the cycle, stir once in a while (adding more broth if it is evaporating too swiftly). When the cooking cycle is complete, mix in the butter and Parmigiano.
2. Move the polenta to a platter and position the peppers and sausages over the polenta before you serve.

Sweet Sausage and Broccoli Rabe With Farro

Ingredients:

- ½ cup/80 g finely chopped red onion
- ½ cup/85 g golden raisins
- ⅔ cup/165 ml white wine (Sauvignon Blanc or Pinot Grigio)
- ¾ lb/340 g bulk Italian sweet sausage
- 1 bunch broccoli rabe, tough stems removed, finely chopped
- 1 cup/200 g pearled farro

- 1 cup/240 ml chicken or vegetable broth
- 2 garlic cloves, minced
- 2 Tbsp extra-virgin olive oil
- Grated zest of 1 lemon
- Salt and freshly ground black pepper

Directions:

1. Put the farro in a sieve and wash under a stable stream of cool water, stirring the grains. Once the water appears to run clear, stop washing and shake the sieve to drain off surplus water.

2. Set a moderate-sized rice cooker to the regular cycle or to quick cook if using a fuzzy-logic machine. Heat the olive oil, put in the garlic, and sauté for a minute. Put in the broccoli rabe and sauté for about three minutes, or until tender. Take away the broccoli rabe from the rice cooker, sprinkle with salt and pepper, and save for later. Put in the sausage to the rice cooker and sauté until it loses its pink color.

3. Remove all but 1 Tbsp of oil from the pan. Put in the onion and lemon zest and sauté for another three minutes, or until the onion starts to become tender. Put in the farro, stirring up any bits on the bottom of the cooker. Put in the wine and broth and stir until blended.

4. Secure the lid and reset to the regular cycle. At the end of the cooking cycle, mix in the reserved broccoli rabe and any cooking liquid that has collected. Put in the

raisins, re-cover, and carry on steaming for another five minutes on the keep-warm setting or with the machine turned off. If you own a fuzzy-logic rice cooker, this will be taken care of automatically. Serve warm.

Veal Meatballs Over Rice With Butternut Squash

Ingredients:

Meatballs

- ¼ cup/60 ml milk
- ¼ cup/fifteen g finely chopped fresh flat-leaf parsley
- ½ big sweet yellow onion, such as Vidalia, finely chopped
- ½ tsp freshly ground black pepper
- 1 big egg, beaten
- 1 cup/55 g torn fresh bread
- 1 lb/455 g ground veal
- 1½ tsp salt
- Extra-virgin olive oil for frying

Rice

- ½ big sweet yellow onion, such as Vidalia, finely chopped
- ½ cup/60 g freshly grated Parmigiano-Reggiano cheese
- 1 Tbsp extra-virgin olive oil

- 1½ cups/340 g peeled and finely diced butternut squash
- 2 cups/430 g long-grain rice
- 2 Tbsp unsalted butter
- 2 tsp finely chopped fresh sage leaves
- 3 cups/720 ml chicken or vegetable broth

Directions:

TO MAKE THE MEATBALLS:

1. Place the bread into a big mixing container and pour the milk over the bread. Let stand for five minutes, or until the milk is absorbed. Put in the veal, onion, parsley, salt, pepper, and egg and stir to meticulously combine. Using a portion scoop, shape the mixture into 1-in/2.5-cm balls. In a big frying pan, heat ½ in/12 mm of olive oil and brown the meatballs on all sides, in batches.

2. Drain over paper towels. Position the meatballs in the steamer basket—you may have to stack them—and save for later. (At this point, you can cool the meatballs, place in your fridge them for maximum 8 hours, and then proceed with the recipe.)

TO MAKE THE RICE:

1. Put the rice in a sieve and wash under a stable stream of cool water, stirring the grains. Once the water appears to run clear, stop washing and shake the sieve to drain off surplus water.

2. Set a moderate-sized rice cooker to the regular cycle or to quick cook if using a fuzzy-logic machine. Melt the butter with the olive oil; put in the onion, sage, and butternut squash; and sauté for three to four minutes, or until the onion becomes tender. Put in the rice and stir until blended. Gradually mix in the chicken broth. Position the steamer basket over the rice. Secure the lid and reset to the regular cycle. At the end of the cooking cycle, remove the steamer basket, stir the Parmigiano into the rice, and move to a platter. Position the meatballs on top of the rice or around the outside of the platter to serve.

Seafood

Baja Cod With Green Rice

Ingredients:

- ¼ cup/60 ml fresh lime juice, plus 1 Tbsp
- ½ tsp ground cumin
- 1½ cups/315 g long-grain white rice
- 1½ lb/680 g cod fillets
- 2 cups/480 ml pale Mexican beer
- 2 Tbsp chopped fresh cilantro, plus ¼ cup/fifteen g finely chopped

- 3 green onions, white and soft green parts, finely chopped
- 3 Tbsp extra-virgin olive oil
- Spicy Cabbage Slaw (recipe follows) for serving (not necessary)

Directions:

1. Put the cod fillets in a big zipper-top plastic bag. In a small container, whisk together 2 Tbsp of the olive oil, the ¼ cup/60 ml lime juice, 2 Tbsp cilantro, and cumin. Pour the mixture over the cod, seal the bag, and marinate in your fridge for minimum 2 hours, or maximum 6 hours.

2. Put the rice in a sieve and wash under a stable stream of cool water, stirring the grains. Once the water appears to run clear, stop washing and shake the sieve to drain off surplus water.

3. Place the rice in a moderate-sized rice cooker and put in the beer, rest of the 1 Tbsp lime juice, and rest of the 1 Tbsp olive oil, stirring to combine. Close the lid and cook using regular cycle. Set a timer for about twenty minutes. Once the timer finishes, drain the cod, discarding the marinade, and put the cod in the steamer basket over the rice. Continue with the cooking cycle. At the end of the cooking cycle, check the fish to ensure that it is thoroughly cooked (it must be opaque and register 145°F/63°C on an instant-read thermometer).

4. Re-cover the rice cooker and let the fish and rice carry on steaming for another ten minutes on the keep-warm setting or with the machine turned off. If you own a fuzzy-logic rice cooker, this will be taken care of automatically. Take away the fish from the rice cooker. Fluff the rice and mix in the green onions and rest of the ¼ cup/fifteen g cilantro. Mound the rice on a platter and put the fish on top. Serve the cabbage slaw on the side, if you wish.

SPICY CABBAGE SLAW

Ingredients:

- ¼ cup/60 ml fresh orange juice
- ¼ cup/fifteen g finely chopped fresh cilantro
- ½ cup/120 ml rice vinegar
- ½ cup/70 g thinly cut red cabbage
- ½ tsp freshly ground black pepper
- ¾ cup/180 ml extra-virgin olive oil
- 1 head green cabbage, cored and thinly cut
- 1 medium carrot, peeled and crudely grated
- 1/8 tsp Tabasco or your favorite hot sauce
- 1½ tsp salt

Directions:

1. Put both cabbages and the carrot in a big mixing container. In a small mixing container, whisk together the rice vinegar, orange juice, olive oil, salt, pepper, and Tabasco. (Taste for seasoning and adjust if required.)
2. Pour the dressing over the vegetables and stir to combine. Put in the cilantro and toss once more. Serve instantly or cover and place in your fridge for maximum 8 hours.

Beer-Steamed Shrimp With Lemon Farro

Ingredients:

- ½ to 1 cup/1fifteen to 225 g unsalted butter, melted
- 1 cup/200 g pearled farro
- 1 Tbsp Old Bay Seasoning
- 1⅓ cups/315 ml chicken or vegetable broth
- 2 garlic cloves, minced
- 2 lb/910 g big shrimp
- 2 Tbsp extra-virgin olive oil
- An assortment of hot sauces for serving
- One 12-oz/360-ml bottle beer
- Salt and freshly ground black pepper
- Zest of 4 lemons, ⅔ cup/165 ml fresh lemon juice, plus lemon wedges for decorate

Directions:

1. In a big container, mix the shrimp, Old Bay, half the lemon zest, lemon juice, and beer. Cover and place in your fridge at least 2 hours, or maximum 8 hours.
2. Put the farro in a sieve and wash under a stable stream of cool water, stirring the grains. Once the water appears to run clear, stop washing and shake the sieve to drain off surplus water.
3. Set a moderate-sized rice cooker to the regular cycle or to quick cook if using a fuzzy-logic machine. Heat the olive oil, put in the garlic and farro, and sauté for a

minute to toast the farro. Slowly pour in the chicken broth.

4. Secure the lid and reset to the regular cycle. Set a timer for about twenty minutes. In the meantime, drain the shrimp and position in the steamer basket; you may have to stack them. Once the timer finishes, check the farro (add a little extra broth if required) and put the steamer basket over the farro.

5. Secure the lid and reset the timer for about ten minutes. Once the timer finishes, the shrimp must be pink and thoroughly cookedout, and the farro must be soft but still firm to the bite (firm to the bite). Flavour the farro with salt and pepper, if required. Mix in the rest of the lemon zest. Move the farro to a big serving container, and put the shrimp in a different container. Serve the shrimp with the melted butter for dipping, the lemon wedges, and the hot sauces.

Cajun Salmon With Dirty Rice and Fruit Salsa

Ingredients:

- ¼ cup/40 g finely chopped green bell pepper
- ¼ cup/60 ml extra-virgin olive oil
- ½ lb/225 g pork breakfast sausages, removed from their casings

- 1 medium onion, finely chopped
- 1½ lb/675 g salmon fillets
- 2 celery ribs, finely chopped
- 2 cups/430 g long-grain rice
- 2 garlic cloves, minced
- 2 Tbsp Cajun Seasoning, homemade (recipe follows) or store bought
- 2 tsp dried thyme leaves
- 3 cups/720 ml chicken broth
- Fruit Salsa for serving
- Pinch of cayenne pepper

Directions:

1. Put the rice in a sieve and wash under a stable stream of cool water, stirring the grains. Once the water appears to run clear, stop washing and shake the sieve to drain off surplus water.
2. In a small container, mix the olive oil and Cajun seasoning. Paint the salmon on both sides with the oil mixture and save for later.
3. Set a moderate-sized rice cooker to the regular cycle or to quick cook if using a fuzzy-logic machine. Cook the sausage until it is no longer pink. Discard all but 1 Tbsp of the fat in the rice cooker. Put in the onion, celery, bell pepper, garlic, cayenne, and thyme and sauté for two to three minutes; the vegetables will be aromatic. Put in the rice and chicken broth. Reset the rice cooker to the

regular cycle and set a timer for about ten minutes. Once the timer finishes, position the salmon in the steamer basket, and place over the rice.

4. Secure the lid and continue with the cooking cycle. At the end of the cooking cycle, check the salmon to ensure it is thoroughly cooked (it should show 145°F/63°C on an instant-read thermometer). Take away the fish from the rice cooker and let the rice carry on steaming for another five minutes on the keep-warm setting or with the machine turned off. If you own a fuzzy-logic rice cooker, this will be taken care of automatically. Move the rice to a big platter and put the salmon on top. Place the fruit salsa in a decorative container and serve it alongside the fish and rice.

CAJUN SEASONING

Yield: ½ CUP/70 G

Ingredients:

- ½ tsp freshly ground black pepper
- ½ tsp ground white pepper
- 1 Tbsp garlic powder
- 1 Tbsp onion powder
- 1 Tbsp sweet paprika
- 1 tsp cayenne pepper
- 1 tsp dried oregano leaves
- 2 tsp dried thyme leaves
- 3 Tbsp sea salt

Directions:

1. In a big container, mix the sea salt, paprika, onion powder, garlic powder, cayenne, white pepper, black pepper, thyme, and oregano.
2. Move to an airtight container. Store in a cool, dry place for maximum half a year.

FRUIT SALSA

Yield: 2 CUPS/360 G

Ingredients:

- ½ cup/80 g finely chopped red or yellow bell pepper
- ½ cup/80 g finely diced red onion
- ½ tsp salt
- 1 tsp finely diced jalapeño chile
- 1½ cups/240 g finely diced peeled fresh fruit
- 2 Tbsp extra-virgin olive oil
- 2 Tbsp finely chopped fresh cilantro or flat-leaf parsley
- 2 Tbsp fresh lemon, orange, or lime juice, or rice vinegar
- 3 or 4 dashes hot sauce (not necessary)

Directions:

1. Mix the fruit, red onion, bell pepper, jalapeño, cilantro, lemon juice, olive oil, salt, and hot sauce (if using) together in a moderate-sized mixing container.
2. Cover and place in your fridge for minimum 2 hours, or maximum 3 days.

Curried Shrimp With Basmati Rice

Ingredients:

- ½ cup/30 g finely chopped fresh cilantro
- ½ tsp curry powder
- ½ tsp ground turmeric
- 1 cup/215 g basmati rice
- 1 medium onion, finely chopped
- 1 tsp ground coriander
- 1½ lb/680 g medium shrimp, peeled and deveined
- 2 garlic cloves, minced
- 2 Tbsp vegetable oil
- 2 tsp grated peeled fresh ginger
- One 14½-oz/415-g can chopped tomatoes, with their juice
- One 14-oz/420-ml can coconut milk

Directions:

1. Put the rice in a sieve and wash under a stable stream of cool water, stirring the grains. Once the water appears to run clear, stop washing and shake the sieve to drain off surplus water.

2. Set a moderate-sized rice cooker to the regular cycle or to quick cook if using a fuzzy-logic machine. Heat the vegetable oil; put in the garlic, ginger, onion, turmeric, curry powder, and coriander; and sauté for three to four

minutes, or until the onion is translucent and the spices are aromatic. Put in the tomatoes, coconut milk, and rice, stirring to spread the ingredients.

3. Secure the lid and reset to the regular cycle. Set a timer for about twenty minutes. Once the timer finishes, put in the shrimp, close the lid, and switch the machine off. Allow the curry carry on steaming for five minutes. Mix the curry and check to ensure that the shrimp have all turned pink and are thoroughly cooked. If they are not done, re-cover and allow the shrimp to sit for another five minutes. Mix in the cilantro before you serve.

Garlicky Clam Risotto

Ingredients:

- ¼ cup/fifteen g finely chopped fresh flat-leaf parsley
- ½ cup/120 ml dry white wine, such as Sauvignon Blanc or Pinot Grigio
- 1 cup/215 g medium-grain rice, such as Carnaroli or Arborio
- 1 cup/225 g shucked clams, crudely chopped
- 1 cup/240 ml chicken or vegetable broth
- 1½ cups/360 ml clam juice
- 3 Tbsp extra-virgin olive oil
- 6 garlic cloves, minced
- Grated zest of 1 lemon

- Salt and freshly ground black pepper

Directions:

1. Put the rice in a sieve and wash under a stable stream of cool water, stirring the grains. Once the water appears to run clear, stop washing and shake the sieve to drain off surplus water.
2. Set a moderate-sized rice cooker to the regular cycle or to quick cook if using a fuzzy-logic machine. Heat the olive oil, put in the garlic and clams, and sauté for a minute. Put in the rice and stir to coat with the oil mixture. Put in the wine and bring to its boiling point. Gradually put in the chicken broth and clam juice.
3. Secure the lid and reset to the regular cycle. Set a timer for about twenty minutes. Once the timer finishes, check the risotto; the rice must be firm to the bite (still firm to the bite). If it needs a little extra time, re-cover the cooker and allow it to sit for five minutes. Mix in the lemon zest and parsley and sprinkle with salt and pepper before you serve.

Halibut With Lemon-Dill Rice

Ingredients:

- ¼ cup/60 ml extra-virgin olive oil

- ¼ cup/fifteen g finely chopped fresh dill, plus more for decorate
- 1½ lb/680 g halibut fillets
- 2 cups/430 g long-grain rice
- 3 cups/720 ml vegetable broth or water
- 4 Tbsp/55 g unsalted butter, melted
- Grated zest of 2 lemons, plus 2 Tbsp fresh lemon juice

Directions:

1. In a big shallow container, mix the olive oil, butter, lemon zest, and lemon juice. Ladle out ¼ cup/60 ml of the lemony mixture into a small container and save for later. Place the halibut in the shallow container flipping the fish to coat with the rest of the mixture, and save for later.

2. Put the rice in a sieve and wash under a stable stream of cool water, stirring the grains. Once the water appears to run clear, stop washing and shake the sieve to drain off surplus water.

3. Mix the rice and vegetable broth in a moderate-sized rice cooker. Close the lid and cook using regular cycle. Set a timer for about ten minutes. Once the timer finishes, position the halibut in the steamer basket over the rice. Re-cover the rice cooker and carry on cooking until the cycle is complete. The halibut must be thoroughly cooked (it should show 145°F/63°C on an instant-read thermometer). Take away the fish from the

rice cooker and cover with aluminum foil to keep warm. Mix the reserved lemon-butter mixture and the dill into the rice and cover. Allow the rice to carry on steaming for another five minutes on the keep-warm setting or with the machine turned off. If you own a fuzzy-logic rice cooker, this will be taken care of automatically. Move the rice to a platter and put the fish on top. Decorate using more chopped dill before you serve.

Miso Cod Over Black Rice

Ingredients:

- ¼ cup/60 ml sake
- ¼ cup/60 ml white (shiro) miso
- ½ cup/120 ml mirin (Japanese sweet rice wine)
- 1 cup/170 g frozen shelled edamame, defrosted
- 1 Tbsp sugar
- 1 to 2 Tbsp toasted sesame oil
- 1 tsp salt
- 1½ lb/680 g cod fillets, cut into 4 pieces
- 2 cups/430 g black rice
- 2 green onions, white and soft green parts, finely chopped
- 3¾ cups/900 ml water

Directions:

1. Put the cod in a big zipper-top plastic bag. In a small mixing container, whisk together the sake, miso, sugar, and ¼ cup/60 ml of the mirin until mixed. Pour over the cod in the bag, seal, and place in your fridge for minimum 2 hours, or maximum 8 hours. When you are ready to start the rice, drain the marinade into a small deep cooking pan and boil for five minutes. Keep warm while the rice is cooking. Position the cod in the steamer basket of the rice cooker and save for later.

2. Put the rice in a sieve and wash under a stable stream of cool water, stirring the grains. Once the water appears to run clear, stop washing and shake the sieve to drain off surplus water.

3. Mix the rice, 3¾ cups/900 ml water, rest of the ¼ cup/60 ml mirin, and the salt in a moderate-sized rice cooker. Close the lid and cook using regular cycle. Set a timer for about twenty minutes. Once the timer finishes, remove the lid and position the steamer basket over the rice. Re-cover the rice cooker and cook for an extra ten minutes. Ensure that the cod is thoroughly cooked (it should show 145°F/63°C on an instant-read thermometer). Fluff the rice and move to a big platter. Position the cod on top of the rice and sprinkle with the warm marinade. Decorate using a sprinkle of toasted sesame oil and drizzle with the green onions and edamame before you serve.

Miso-Glazed Sea Bass Over Quinoa With Vegetables

Ingredients:

- ¼ cup/40 g finely chopped red onion
- ¼ cup/50 g sugar
- ¼ cup/55 g white (shiro) miso
- ¼ cup/60 ml mirin (Japanese sweet rice wine)
- ½ cup/80 g finely chopped red bell pepper
- ½ cup/85 g corn kernels, cut fresh from the cob, or frozen kernels, defrosted
- 1 medium zucchini, finely diced
- 1 Tbsp extra-virgin olive oil
- 1½ cups/280 g prewashed quinoa
- 2 Tbsp soy sauce
- 2¼ cups/540 ml chicken or vegetable broth
- Four 4- to 6-oz/115- to 170-g sea bass fillets
- Toasted sesame oil for decorate

Directions:

1. In a small container, whisk together the sugar, mirin, miso, and soy sauce. Place the fish on a plate and pour the marinade over it. Turn the fish to coat and place in your fridge for minimum half an hour, or maximum 2 hours.

2. Set a moderate-sized rice cooker to the regular cycle or to quick cook if using a fuzzy-logic machine. Heat the olive oil, put in the red onion, and cook for about three minutes, or until the onion becomes tender. Put in the zucchini, bell pepper, and corn and toss with the oil. Put in the quinoa and chicken broth and stir until blended. Drain the sea bass, discarding the marinade. Position the fish in a steamer basket and place over the quinoa.

3. Secure the lid and reset to the regular cycle. At the end of the cooking cycle, fluff the quinoa and ensure the fish is thoroughly cooked (it should show 145°F/63°C on an instant-read thermometer). If it still needs some time, cover the machine and allow the residual heat to cook the fish. Move the quinoa to a platter and put the sea bass on top. Decorate using a sprinkle of sesame oil before you serve.

New Orleans–Style Barbecue Shrimp With Cheese and Bacon Grits

Ingredients:

Grits

- 1 cup/140 g coarse stone-ground grits
- 1 tsp salt
- 1¼ cups/300 ml chicken or vegetable broth

- 1½ cups/170 g finely shredded sharp white cheddar cheese
- 1½ cups/360 ml whole milk
- 2 or 3 dashes Tabasco sauce
- 4 strips bacon, cooked until crunchy and crumbled

Shrimp

- ¼ cup/60 ml fresh lemon juice
- ¼ cup/fifteen g chopped fresh flat-leaf parsley
- ½ cup/115 g unsalted butter
- ½ tsp dried thyme
- ½ tsp sweet paprika
- 1 Tbsp extra-virgin olive oil
- 1 tsp dried oregano
- 1/8 tsp freshly ground black pepper
- 1½ lb/680 g big shrimp, peeled and deveined
- 2 Tbsp Worcestershire sauce
- 4 garlic cloves, minced
- Pinch of cayenne pepper

Directions:

TO MAKE THE GRITS:

1. Coat the interior of a moderate-sized rice cooker with nonstick cooking spray. Put in the grits, chicken broth,

milk, and salt, stirring to blend. Close the lid and cook using regular cycle.

2. During the cycle (which may take up to half an hour), stir the grits a few times. (If you need more liquid near the end of the cooking time, mix in a little broth or milk.) When the grits are done, mix in the bacon, cheese, and Tabasco.

TO MAKE THE SHRIMP:

1. When the grits are about midway through their cooking cycle, in a big frying pan, melt the butter with the olive oil on moderate heat and cook the garlic, stirring, until tender, approximately 3 minutes.

2. Put in the oregano, thyme, paprika, black pepper, and cayenne and cook for an extra two minutes, stirring so the spices do not burn. Put in the Worcestershire and lemon juice and simmer for a minute. Put in the shrimp and cook, stirring, until they turn completely pink, approximately eight minutes.

3. Move the grits to a platter or individual bowls and top with the barbecue shrimp. Decorate using the parsley before you serve.

Paella

Ingredients:

- ¼ cup/60 ml dry white wine, such as Sauvignon Blanc or Pinot Grigio
- ¼ cup/fifteen g finely chopped fresh flat-leaf parsley
- ½ cup/105 g finely chopped Spanish chorizo or sopressata
- ½ cup/80 g finely chopped red onion
- ½ lb/225 g medium shrimp, peeled and deveined
- ½ tsp saffron threads, crushed in the palm of your hand
- 1 boneless, skinless chicken breast half (5 to 6 oz/140 to 170 g), finely chopped
- 1 cup/215 g medium-grain rice, such as Carnaroli or Arborio
- 1 cup/85 g shelled English peas, or frozen peas, defrosted
- 1 lemon, cut into wedges
- 1 medium red bell pepper, cored, seeded, and finely chopped
- 1 Tbsp extra-virgin olive oil
- 12 small clams in their shells, scrubbed
- 2½ cups/600 ml chicken or vegetable broth
- 3 garlic cloves, minced
- One 14½-oz/415-g can chopped tomatoes, with their juice

Directions:

1. Put the rice in a sieve and wash under a stable stream of cool water, stirring the grains. Once the water appears to run clear, stop washing and shake the sieve to drain off surplus water.

2. Set a moderate-sized rice cooker to the regular cycle or to quick cook if using a fuzzy-logic machine. Heat the olive oil and sauté the chicken until it is white on all sides (it will cook through during the cooking cycle). Put in the chorizo, onion, garlic, and bell pepper and sauté for about three minutes, or until the onion starts to tenderize and the garlic is aromatic. Pour the wine into a small measuring cup and drizzle the saffron over it. Put in the tomatoes to the cooker, pour in the broth and wine, and bring to its boiling point. Mix in the rice.

3. Secure the lid and reset to the regular cycle. Set a timer for about twenty minutes. Once the timer finishes, there should still be liquid left in the pan. Position the clams in the steamer basket, with the hinges facing up. Mix the shrimp and peas into the rice. Put the steamer basket above the rice, close the lid, and set the timer for five minutes. Once the timer finishes, check to ensure the clams have opened. If they haven't, close the lid, turn off the machine, and set the timer for another five minutes. At that point, discard any clams that haven't opened.

4. Take away the steamer basket and stir the rice. Move the rice to a big shallow container, position the clams around the container, and decorate with the lemon

wedges. Drizzle the paella with the parsley before you serve.

Parchment-Steamed Sea Bass Veracruz Over Cilantro Quinoa

Ingredients:

- ¼ cup/60 ml extra-virgin olive oil
- ¼ tsp freshly ground black pepper
- ½ cup/30 g finely chopped fresh cilantro or flat-leaf parsley
- ½ tsp ground cumin
- ½ tsp salt
- 1 Anaheim chile, seeded, deribbed, and finely chopped
- 1 Hass avocado, pitted, peeled, and thinly cut
- 1 medium white onion, finely chopped
- 1½ cups/230 g cherry tomatoes, quartered
- 1½ cups/280 g prewashed quinoa
- 1½ lb/680 g sea bass fillets, cut into 4 portions
- 2 Tbsp fresh lime juice
- 2½ cups/600 ml chicken or vegetable broth

Directions:

1. Cut four pieces of parchment paper into 10-by-12-in/25-by-30.5-cm rectangles. Place a piece of sea bass in the

middle of each piece of parchment. In a mixing container, mix together the tomatoes, onion, chile, cumin, olive oil, and lime juice. Top each piece of fish with some of the tomato-onion mixture. If you have extra, save it to decorate the quinoa. Fold the paper over the fish, and seal the edges by folding them over a few times to make a trim package. Stack the fish packages in the steamer basket of the rice cooker and save for later.

2. Place the quinoa in a moderate-sized rice cooker and mix in the chicken broth, salt, and pepper. Position the steamer basket over the quinoa. Secure the lid and set to the regular cycle. At the end of the cooking cycle, check the fish to ensure it is thoroughly cooked (it should show 145°F/63°C on an instant-read thermometer). Allow the fish and quinoa to carry on steaming for another five minutes on the keep-warm setting or with the machine turned off. If you own a fuzzy-logic rice cooker, this will be taken care of automatically. Fluff the quinoa and mix in ¼ cup/fifteen g of the cilantro. Move the quinoa to a serving container. Open each packet of fish, lay a few slices of avocado over the fish, and drizzle with the rest of the cilantro. Plate the fish packets before you serve.

Parsley Pesto Halibut Over White Risotto

Ingredients:

Pesto

- ¼ cup/60 ml white wine or dry vermouth
- ⅓ cup/45 g freshly grated Parmigiano-Reggiano cheese
- ½ cup/60 g freshly grated Parmigiano-Reggiano cheese
- ½ cup/80 g finely chopped sweet onion, such as Vidalia
- ½ to ⅔ cup/120 to 165 ml extra-virgin olive oil
- 1 cup/115 g walnuts
- 1 cup/60 g packed fresh flat-leaf parsley leaves
- 1 Tbsp capers in brine, drained
- 1 Tbsp extra-virgin olive oil
- 1½ lb/680 g halibut fillets
- 2 cups/430 g long-grain rice
- 2 garlic cloves, peeled
- 2⅔ cups/630 ml chicken broth
- 4 Tbsp/55 g unsalted butter

Directions:

1. ***TO MAKE THE PESTO:*** In a food processor or blender, mix the parsley, walnuts, garlic, Parmigiano, and capers, pulsing to break up the nuts. While the machine runs, add ½ cup/120 ml of the olive oil. This must be a paste, not a runny pesto. Put in slightly more oil if required. Remove from the machine and pour into an airtight container, spooning one to 2 Tbsp olive oil over the top of the pesto to preserve its green color. You should have approximately 1½ to 2 cups/350 to 470 g. Set aside 1

cup/235 g for the halibut. Place in your fridge the rest for maximum one week or freeze for maximum three months.

2. Put the rice in a sieve and wash under a stable stream of cool water, stirring the grains. Once the water appears to run clear, stop washing and shake the sieve to drain off surplus water.

3. Set a moderate-sized rice cooker to the regular cycle or to quick cook if using a fuzzy-logic machine, and melt 2 Tbsp of the butter with the olive oil. Sauté the onion for about three minutes, or until it starts to become tender. Put in the wine, rice, and chicken broth.

4. Secure the lid and reset to the regular cycle. Set a timer for about ten minutes. Once the timer finishes, paint the halibut fillets with the pesto and position in a steamer basket. Put in the rice cooker and cover. Set the timer one more time for about ten minutes. At the end of the cooking time, the halibut must be thoroughly cooked (it should show 145°F/63°C on an instant-read thermometer), and the rice should still have a small amount of liquid in it.

5. Take away the halibut from the rice cooker and cover with aluminum foil to keep warm. Mix the rest of the 2 Tbsp butter and the Parmigiano into the rice. Cover and allow to carry on steaming for another five minutes on the keep-warm setting or with the machine turned off. If you own a fuzzy-logic rice cooker, this will be taken care

of automatically. At this point the risotto must be firm to the bite (firm to the bite), and there should still be a small amount of liquid left in the pan. Move the risotto to a platter, put the halibut on top, before you serve.

Scampi With Brown Rice Pilaf

Ingredients:

- ¼ cup/fifteen g finely chopped fresh flat-leaf parsley
- ½ cup/115 g unsalted butter
- ½ cup/120 ml dry white wine, such as Sauvignon Blanc or Pinot Grigio
- ½ cup/80 g finely chopped sweet yellow onion, such as Vidalia
- 1 Tbsp finely chopped fresh oregano
- 1½ lb/680 g big shrimp, peeled and deveined
- 2 cups/430 g brown rice
- 3½ cups/840 ml chicken or vegetable broth
- 4 Tbsp/60 ml extra-virgin olive oil
- 6 garlic cloves, minced
- Grated zest of 3 lemons

Directions:

1. Put the rice in a sieve and wash under a stable stream of cool water, stirring the grains. Once the water appears

to run clear, stop washing and shake the sieve to drain off surplus water.

2. Set a moderate-sized rice cooker to the regular cycle or to quick cook if using a fuzzy-logic machine. Heat 2 Tbsp of the olive oil and sauté the onion and two-thirds of the lemon zest for a minute, or until the lemon zest is aromatic. Put in the rice and toast in the oil for a minute. Slowly put in the chicken broth.

3. Secure the lid and reset to the regular cycle. Set a timer for about twenty minutes. In the meantime, stack the shrimp in the steamer basket and save for later. In a small sauté pan, melt the butter with the rest of the 2 Tbsp olive oil and sauté the garlic, oregano, and rest of the lemon zest until the garlic is aromatic, approximately 2 minutes. Put in the wine and bring to its boiling point. Put in the parsley and remove the garlic butter from the heat.

4. Once the timer finishes, position the steamer basket over the rice. Set the timer for about ten minutes. Rewarm the garlic butter. Once the timer finishes again, the rice must be soft, and the shrimp must be pink and thoroughly cooked. Take away the steamer basket and move the rice to a platter. Position the shrimp over the rice and sprinkle the garlic butter over the shrimp. Serve instantly.

Soy-Marinated Salmon With Bok Choy and Coconut Rice

Ingredients:

Salmon

- ¼ cup/fifteen g finely chopped fresh cilantro
- ½ cup/120 ml rice vinegar
- ½ cup/120 ml soy sauce
- ½ cup/120 ml water
- 1 head bok choy
- 1 tsp chili-garlic sauce
- 2 Tbsp dark brown sugar
- 2 Tbsp seeded and finely chopped jalapeño chile
- 2 tsp fresh lime juice
- Four ½-lb/225-g salmon fillets

Coconut Rice

- 1 cup/240 ml coconut milk
- 1 cup/240 ml water
- 1⅓ cups/280 g basmati rice

Directions:

TO MAKE THE SALMON:

1. In a small mixing container, whisk together the soy sauce, water, rice vinegar, brown sugar, chili-garlic sauce, cilantro, lime juice, and jalapeño. Place the salmon into a big zipper-top plastic bag and pour the marinade over the salmon. Seal the bag and place in your fridge for minimum 2 hours, and up to 6 hours.
2. Chop off the root end of the bok choy and separate the leaves. Put on a microwavable plate and cover with damp paper towels. Microwave on high until the bok choy is flexible, approximately 1½ minutes. Set aside to cool.
3. Take away the salmon from the marinade and pour the marinade into a small deep cooking pan. Bring to its boiling point and continue boiling for five minutes. Reduce the heat and simmer until the marinade has a syrupy consistency, approximately fifteen minutes more. Cover each piece of salmon in a leaf of bok choy, securing it using a toothpick or a silicone band. Cut the rest of the bok choy into ½-in/12-mm ribbons and line the steamer basket with the chopped bok choy. Stack the salmon packets on top and save for later.

TO MAKE THE COCONUT RICE:

1. Put the rice in a sieve and wash under a stable stream of cool water, stirring the grains. Once the water appears to run clear, stop washing and shake the sieve to drain off surplus water.

2. Place the rice in a moderate-sized rice cooker and mix in the coconut milk and 1 cup/240 ml water. Close the lid and cook using regular cycle. Set a timer for about ten minutes. Once the timer finishes, put the steamer basket over the rice, cover, and carry on cooking. At the end of the cooking cycle, check to ensure the salmon is thoroughly cooked (it must be opaque and register 145°F/63°C on an instant-read thermometer).

3. Re-cover the rice cooker and allow the rice and salmon to carry on steaming for another ten minutes on the keep-warm setting or with the machine turned off. If you own a fuzzy-logic rice cooker, this will be taken care of automatically. In the meantime, rewarm the marinade, which is now a sauce. Mound the rice on a platter, remove the toothpicks or silicone bands from the salmon packets, and position the salmon on top of the rice. Distribute the chopped bok choy around the edges of the platter and sprinkle a small amount of the sauce over the bok choy and the salmon packets. Serve the rest of the sauce warm on the side.

Sweet and Pungent Shrimp and Broccoli With Steamed Rice

Ingredients:

- ¼ cup/50 g sugar

- ¼ cup/60 ml ketchup
- 1 Tbsp mirin (Japanese sweet rice wine)
- 1 Tbsp soy sauce
- 1 tsp grated peeled fresh ginger
- 1 tsp red pepper flakes
- 1 tsp salt
- 1½ cups/315 g short-grain rice
- 1½ lb/680 g big shrimp, peeled and deveined
- 1¾ cups/420 ml water
- 2 cups/320 g broccoli florets
- 2 garlic cloves, minced
- 2 green onions, white and soft green parts, finely chopped (not necessary)
- 3 Tbsp rice vinegar

Directions:

1. In a small container, whisk together the sugar, ketchup, soy sauce, rice vinegar, mirin, garlic, ginger, and red pepper flakes. Put in the shrimp and toss to coat. Cover and place in your fridge for maximum 2 hours.
2. Put the rice in a sieve and wash under a stable stream of cool water, stirring the grains. Once the water appears to run clear, stop washing and shake the sieve to drain off surplus water.
3. Place the rice in a moderate-sized rice cooker. Cover with the 1¾ cups/420 ml water and put in the salt. Close

the lid and cook using regular cycle. Set a timer for fifteen minutes. In the meantime, position the broccoli in the steamer basket and top with the shrimp. Once the timer finishes, position the steamer basket over the rice.

4. Re-cover the rice cooker and carry on cooking until the end of the cycle (about ten minutes more). When the rice is cooked, ensure the shrimp have thoroughly cooked and turned pink and the broccoli is soft. Allow the rice to carry on steaming for another ten minutes on the keep-warm setting or with the machine turned off. If you own a fuzzy-logic rice cooker, this will be taken care of automatically. Take away the steamer basket, fluff the rice, and mound the rice on a platter. Top with the shrimp and broccoli, and serve decorated with the chopped green onions, if you wish, before you serve.

Vegetables and Grains

Asparagus and Goat Cheese Frittata

Ingredients:

- ¼ tsp Tabasco sauce
- ⅓ cup/75 ml heavy cream
- ½ cup/30 g crumbled goat cheese

- ½ lb/225 g asparagus, trimmed and slice into ½-in/12-mm pieces
- 1 Tbsp finely chopped spring onion or green onion, white part only
- 1 Tbsp olive oil
- 1 tsp salt
- 4 big eggs

Directions:

1. Set a moderate-sized rice cooker to the regular cycle or to quick cook if using a fuzzy-logic machine. Heat the olive oil and sauté the spring onion for a minute. Put in the asparagus and cook for an extra three minutes, or until the asparagus starts to become tender. In a moderate-sized mixing container, whisk together the eggs, cream, salt, and Tabasco. Pour the egg mixture over the asparagus and drizzle with the goat cheese.
2. Secure the lid and reset to the regular cycle. The frittata will take three to four minutes to cook. Let it carry on steaming, covered, for another six minutes on the keep-warm setting or with the machine turned off. If you own a fuzzy-logic rice cooker, this will be taken care of automatically. Serve warm or at room temperature.

Baby Artichoke Farro Pilaf

Ingredients:

- ½ cup/120 ml dry white wine, such as Sauvignon Blanc or Pinot Grigio, or dry vermouth
- ½ cup/80 g finely chopped shallots
- ⅔ cup/165 ml chicken or vegetable broth
- 1 bay leaf
- 1 cup/200 g pearled farro
- 1 Tbsp extra-virgin olive oil
- 1 tsp dried thyme
- 2 garlic cloves, minced
- 2 Tbsp finely chopped fresh flat-leaf parsley
- 2 Tbsp unsalted butter
- 4 baby artichokes, trimmed and quartered
- Grated zest of 2 lemons, plus ½ cup/120 ml fresh lemon juice

Directions:

1. Put the farro in a sieve and wash under a stable stream of cool water, stirring the grains. Once the water appears to run clear, stop washing and shake the sieve to drain off surplus water.
2. Set a moderate-sized rice cooker to the regular cycle or to quick cook if using a fuzzy-logic machine. Melt the butter with the olive oil, put in the shallots and garlic, and sauté for a couple of minutes, or until the shallots start to become tender. Put in the artichokes, lemon

zest, thyme, and bay leaf. Sauté the artichokes for three to four minutes, turning regularly to coat with the butter mixture. Put in the farro and toast the farro for a couple of minutes. Slowly pour in the lemon juice, white wine, and chicken broth.

3. Secure the lid and reset to the regular cycle. When the pilaf is done, check to ensure the artichoke hearts are soft. If they aren't fairly done, re-cover and carry on steaming for five to ten minutes on the keep-warm setting or with the cooker turned off. If you own a fuzzy-logic rice cooker, this will be taken care of automatically. Take away the bay leaf, move the pilaf to a big container, and decorate with the parsley before you serve.

Barley Salad With Pancetta, Corn, and Curry Vinaigrette

Ingredients:

Curry Dressing

- ¼ cup/fifteen g finely chopped fresh chives, plus whole chives for decorate
- ⅓ cup/65 g sugar
- ½ cup/120 ml red wine vinegar
- ½ cup/120 ml vegetable oil
- ½ tsp dry mustard

- ½ tsp garlic salt
- 1 butterhead lettuce, leaves separated
- 1 European cucumber, finely diced
- 1 Tbsp extra-virgin olive oil
- 1 tsp curry powder
- 1 tsp Worcestershire sauce
- 2 cups/340 g corn kernels, cut fresh from the cob, or frozen kernels, defrosted
- 2 tsp fresh lemon juice
- 3 cups/690 g freshly cooked barley
- One ½-in-/12-mm-thick slice pancetta, finely chopped

Directions:

1. ***TO MAKE THE CURRY DRESSING:*** In a mixing container, whisk together the sugar, vinegar, vegetable oil, lemon juice, Worcestershire, curry powder, garlic salt, and dry mustard until mixed. Set aside or place in your fridge for maximum one week.

2. While the barley is still warm, move it to a big serving container and mix in ⅓ cup/75 ml of the dressing. Set aside. In a moderate-sized frying pan, heat the olive oil on moderate to high heat and cook the pancetta until it is crunchy. Remove to paper towels to cool and drain. In the same frying pan, sauté the corn for two to three minutes, until it softens. Put in the cooled pancetta and the corn to the barley and toss in the cucumber and chopped chives. Sprinkle some of the dressing over the

top of the salad and toss again, putting in more dressing if required. Serve the salad in lettuce cups, decorated with whole chives.

Beer-Steamed Rice With Black Beans, Corn, and Tomatoes

Ingredients:

- ¼ cup/fifteen g chopped fresh cilantro
- ½ cup/80 g chopped green bell pepper
- ½ cup/80 g chopped red onion
- ½ tsp dried oregano
- ½ tsp ground cumin
- 1 cup/155 g cherry or pear tomatoes, quartered, or grape tomatoes, halved
- 1 cup/225 g crumbled *queso fresco*
- 1 cup/240 ml sour cream
- 1 Hass avocado, pitted, peeled, and cut
- 1 jalapeño chile, seeded, deribbed, and finely chopped
- 1½ cups/255 g corn kernels, cut fresh from the cob, or frozen kernels, defrosted
- 2 cups/430 g brown basmati or long-grain white rice
- 2 garlic cloves, minced
- 2 Tbsp vegetable oil
- 3 cups/720 ml pale Mexican beer or vegetable broth

- One 14½-oz/415-g can black beans, washed and drained

Directions:

1. Put the rice in a sieve and wash under a stable stream of cool water, stirring the grains. Once the water appears to run clear, stop washing and shake the sieve to drain off surplus water.

2. Set a moderate-sized rice cooker to the regular cycle or to quick cook if using a fuzzy-logic machine. Heat the vegetable oil, put in the garlic and onion, and sauté for a couple of minutes. Put in the tomatoes, bell pepper, jalapeño, cumin, and oregano and sauté for another two minutes, or until the vegetables start to become tender. Put in the rice and stir to coat with the sauce. Put in the beer.

3. Secure the lid and reset to the regular cycle. At the end of the cooking cycle, stir the rice and put in the black beans and corn. Cover and carry on steaming for another five minutes on the keep-warm setting or with the machine turned off. If you own a fuzzy-logic rice cooker, this will be taken care of automatically. Serve, decorated with avocado, *queso fresco*, sour cream, and cilantro.

Black Kale and Farro With Garlic–Pine Nut Pesto

Ingredients:

Pesto

- ½ cup/120 ml extra-virgin olive oil
- ½ cup/55 g pine nuts
- ½ tsp freshly ground black pepper
- 1 bunch black kale, tough stems trimmed, leaves cut into thin ribbons
- 1 cup/120 g freshly grated Parmigiano-Reggiano cheese
- 1 cup/200 g pearled farro
- 1 tsp salt
- 1⅔ cups/405 ml chicken or vegetable broth
- 2 Tbsp extra-virgin olive oil
- 6 garlic cloves, peeled
- Pinch of red pepper flakes

Directions:

1. ***TO MAKE THE PESTO:*** In a blender or food processor, mix the Parmigiano, pine nuts, red pepper flakes, and garlic. Pulse on and off to break up the nuts and garlic. While the machine runs, slowly put in the olive oil and pulse until the mixture comes together. Store in your fridge for maximum 5 days.

2. Put the farro in a sieve and wash under a stable stream of cool water, stirring the grains. Once the water appears

to run clear, stop washing and shake the sieve to drain off surplus water.

3. Set a moderate-sized rice cooker to the regular cycle or to quick cook if using a fuzzy-logic machine. Heat the olive oil, put in the kale (it will look like it wants to jump out of the pan), and cover the rice cooker. Allow the kale to steam for a couple of minutes and turn using tongs to coat in the oil. When the kale is wilted, put in the farro and toss to coat the grains. Put in the chicken broth, salt, and pepper.

4. Secure the lid and set to the regular cycle. At the end of the cooking cycle, stir the farro and put in ½ cup/115 g of the pesto, stirring to combine. Taste for seasoning and put in more pesto if you wish. Serve warm.

Black Kale, Winter Squash, and Bulgur Pilaf

Ingredients:

- ½ cup/80 g finely chopped sweet yellow onion, such as Vidalia
- 1 bunch black kale, tough stems removed, and leaves cut into thin ribbons
- 1 cup/215 g coarse bulgur
- 1 cup/225 g finely chopped butternut squash (or your favorite winter squash), peeled and seeded
- 2 Tbsp extra-virgin olive oil

- 2 Tbsp unsalted butter
- 3 cups/720 ml chicken or vegetable broth
- 4 garlic cloves, minced
- Grated zest of 1 orange

Directions:

1. Put the bulgur in a sieve and wash under a stable stream of cool water, stirring the grains. Once the water appears to run clear, stop washing and shake the sieve to drain off surplus water.
2. Set a moderate-sized rice cooker to the regular cycle or to quick cook if using a fuzzy-logic machine. Heat the olive oil, put in the garlic and onion, and sauté for about three minutes, or until the onion becomes tender. Put in the kale and squash and sauté for another three to four minutes, until the kale starts to become tender. Put in the orange zest and bulgur and turn in the pan, to coat them with the oil. Put in the chicken broth.
3. Secure the lid and reset to the regular cycle. At the end of the cooking cycle, fluff the bulgur and mix in the butter. Allow the bulgur to carry on steaming for another five minutes on the keep-warm setting or with the machine turned off before you serve.

Broccoli Rabe and Pancetta Bread Pudding

Ingredients:

- ¼ cup/40 g finely chopped onion
- ½ tsp freshly ground black pepper
- 1 cup/240 ml heavy cream
- 1 head broccoli rabe, tough stems removed, finely chopped
- 1½ tsp salt
- 2 garlic cloves, minced
- 2 Tbsp extra-virgin olive oil
- 4 big eggs
- 4 cups/460 g torn Italian or French bread with a tender crust
- One ½-in-/12-mm-thick slice pancetta, finely diced

Directions:

1. Coat the interior of a moderate-sized rice cooker with nonstick cooking spray. Set the rice cooker to the regular cycle or to quick cook if using a fuzzy-logic machine. Heat the olive oil, put in the pancetta, and cook until it becomes crunchy. Put in the garlic and cook for a minute. Put in the onion, broccoli rabe, salt, and pepper and sauté for five to six minutes, until the broccoli rabe becomes tender.

2. Place the bread into a big mixing container. In another container, beat the eggs and cream together. Pour the mixture over the bread and stir until blended. Pour the bread-egg mixture into the rice cooker and stir so that

the bits of vegetable and pancetta are distributed throughout the mixture.

3. Secure the lid and reset to the regular cycle. At the end of the cooking cycle, uncover and allow to rest for fifteen minutes on the keep-warm setting or with the machine turned off. Serve warm.

Bulgur Risotto With Mixed Mushrooms

Ingredients:

- ¼ cup/30 g freshly grated Parmigiano-Reggiano cheese
- ½ cup/120 ml dry white wine, such as Sauvignon Blanc or Pinot Grigio, or dry vermouth
- ¾ lb/340 g mixed mushrooms, such as cremini, shiitake (stems removed), chanterelle, and oyster, crudely chopped
- 1 cup/215 g coarse bulgur
- 1 small onion, finely chopped
- 1 Tbsp extra-virgin olive oil
- 2 garlic cloves, minced
- 2 Tbsp finely chopped fresh flat-leaf parsley
- 3 cups/720 ml chicken or vegetable broth or, better still, mushroom broth
- 4 Tbsp/55 g unsalted butter

Directions:

1. Put the bulgur in a sieve and wash under a stable stream of cool water, stirring the grains. Once the water appears to run clear, stop washing and shake the sieve to drain off surplus water.

2. Set a moderate-sized rice cooker to the regular cycle or to quick cook if using a fuzzy-logic machine. Melt 2 Tbsp of the butter with the olive oil, put in the garlic and onion, and sauté for a couple of minutes. Put in the mushrooms and cook for 4 to five minutes, until they start to color and their liquid starts to evaporate. Put in the bulgur and cook for a couple of minutes. Gradually put in the wine and chicken broth.

3. Secure the lid and reset to the regular cycle. Set a timer for about twenty minutes. Once the timer finishes, check to ensure the bulgur is soft. If not, cover and carry on steaming for another five minutes on the keep-warm setting or with the machine turned off. If you own a fuzzy-logic rice cooker, this will be taken care of automatically. Mix in the rest of the 2 Tbsp butter, the Parmigiano, and parsley before you serve.

Curried Cauliflower, Purple Potatoes, and Basmati Rice With Raita

Ingredients:

- ½ lb/225 g small purple potatoes, halved or quartered

- 1 cup/170 g shelled English peas, or frozen petite peas, defrosted
- 1 cup/215 g basmati rice
- 1 medium red onion, finely chopped
- 1 tsp grated peeled fresh ginger
- 1½ cups/360 ml chicken or vegetable broth
- 2 cups/320 g cauliflower florets
- 2 garlic cloves, minced
- 2 medium carrots, peeled and crudely chopped
- 2 Tbsp extra-virgin olive oil
- 2 tsp Madras curry powder
- Assorted chutneys and lime pickles for serving
- One 14½-oz/415-g can coconut milk
- Raita (recipe follows) for serving

Directions:

1. Put the rice in a sieve and wash under a stable stream of cool water, stirring the grains. Once the water appears to run clear, stop washing and shake the sieve to drain off surplus water.

2. Set a moderate-sized rice cooker to the regular cycle or to quick cook if using a fuzzy-logic machine. Heat the olive oil; put in the onion, garlic, ginger, and curry powder; and sauté for a couple of minutes, or until aromatic. Put in the carrots, cauliflower, and potatoes and turn to coat with the curry powder. Gradually put in

the coconut milk and chicken broth and stir until blended. Fit the steamer basket with a coffee filter or a sheet of paper towel, and put the rice on top. Put the steamer basket in the rice cooker.

3. Secure the lid and reset to the regular cycle. Set a timer for about twenty minutes. Once the timer finishes, check to ensure the potatoes are soft; the tip of a sharp paring knife should go through easily. Ensure that the rice is soft, too. Mix in the peas, cover, and carry on steaming for another five minutes on the keep-warm setting or with the machine turned off. (Many rice cookers, including fuzzy-logic machines, do this automatically.) Move the rice to a serving platter, and spoon the curry over the rice. Serve the curry with the raita and assorted chutneys and lime pickles.

RAITA

A Cooling Yogurt Mix from India!

Yield: 2 CUPS/480 ML

Ingredients:

- ½ tsp salt
- 1 cup/240 ml plain yogurt
- 1 European cucumber, peeled and grated
- 1 garlic clove, minced
- 2 Tbsp chopped fresh mint

- 3 or 4 dashes hot sauce (not necessary)

Directions:

1. Put the cucumber in a sieve or colander and allow to drain for half an hour. Squeeze dry and move to a mixing container. Put in the yogurt, garlic, mint, and salt.
2. Taste for seasoning and put in a few dashes of hot sauce, if you wish. Store, covered, in your fridge for maximum four days. Stir before you serve to combine.

Farro Minestrone

Ingredients:

- ¼ cup/fifteen g finely chopped fresh flat-leaf parsley
- 1 cup/200 g pearled farro
- 1 medium onion, finely chopped
- 2 celery ribs, with their leaves, finely chopped
- 2 medium carrots, peeled and finely chopped
- 2 Tbsp extra-virgin olive oil, plus more for drizzling
- 4 cups/960 ml chicken or vegetable broth
- Salt and freshly ground black pepper

Directions:

1. Put the farro in a sieve and wash under a stable stream of cool water, stirring the grains. Once the water appears

to run clear, stop washing and shake the sieve to drain off surplus water.

2. Set a moderate-sized rice cooker to the regular cycle or to quick cook if using a fuzzy-logic machine. Heat the olive oil; put in the onion, celery, and carrots; and sauté for three to four minutes, or until the onion starts to become tender. Put in the farro and chicken broth.

3. Secure the lid and reset to the regular cycle. Set a timer for about twenty minutes. Once the timer finishes, check to see if the farro has become soft. If it's not fairly done, allow it to sit, covered, on the keep-warm setting or with the machine turned off. Using a soup ladle, remove a ladleful of the farro and vegetables to a container. Purée the remaining soup with an immersion blender. (If you do not have one, cool the soup slightly and use a blender or food processor.) Return the reserved farro and vegetables to the soup. Put in the parsley and sprinkle with salt and pepper. Sprinkle each container of soup with olive oil before you serve.

Garlicky Green Beans With Mixed Vegetable Quinoa Pilaf

Ingredients:

- ½ cup/30 g finely chopped fresh flat-leaf parsley
- ½ cup/60 g freshly grated Parmigiano-Reggiano cheese

- ½ cup/80 g finely chopped sweet yellow onion, such as Vidalia
- ½ cup/85 g corn kernels, cut fresh from the cob, or frozen kernels, defrosted
- ½ cup/85 g shelled English peas, or frozen petite peas, defrosted
- ½ lb/225 g green beans, trimmed and slice into 1-in/2.5-cm pieces
- 1 cup/160 g finely diced zucchini or summer squash
- 1 cup/190 g prewashed quinoa
- 1 tsp grated orange zest
- 2 Tbsp extra-virgin olive oil
- 2¼ cups/540 ml chicken or vegetable broth
- 3 garlic cloves, minced
- Grated zest of 1 lemon

Directions:

1. Position the green beans in the steamer basket and save for later. Set a moderate-sized rice cooker to the regular cycle or to quick cook if using a fuzzy-logic machine. Heat the olive oil and sauté the onion for two to three minutes, or until it starts to become tender. Put in the quinoa and cook for a minute, stirring to coat with the oil mixture. Put in the chicken broth slowly. Position the steamer basket over the quinoa.

2. Secure the lid and reset to the regular cycle. While the quinoa and green beans are cooking, mix the garlic, lemon zest, orange zest, parsley, and Parmigiano in a food processor or blender. Process until the mixture forms a paste and save for later. When the cooking cycle is complete, remove the steamer basket and stir the zucchini, corn, and peas into the quinoa. Cover and carry on steaming for another five minutes on the keep-warm setting or with the machine turned off. If you own a fuzzy-logic rice cooker, this will be taken care of automatically. In the meantime, move the green beans to a mixing container and toss with the gremolata. Move the quinoa to a platter and top with the green beans before you serve.

Grain Salad With Artichokes, Tomatoes, and Fresh Mozzarella

Ingredients:

- ¼ cup/20 g packed fresh basil leaves, finely chopped
- ½ cup/120 ml extra-virgin olive oil
- ½ lb/225 g fresh mozzarella, cut into ½-in/12-mm dice
- ½ tsp freshly ground black pepper
- ½ tsp sugar
- 1 cup/155 g cherry or pear tomatoes, halved, or quartered if large

- 1 garlic clove, minced
- 1 tsp salt
- 2 green onions, white and soft green parts, finely chopped
- 3 cups/495 to 690 g freshly cooked grain of your choice
- 3 Tbsp red wine vinegar
- One 10-oz/280-g package frozen artichoke hearts, defrosted, drained, and crudely chopped

Directions:

1. Place the warm grain in a big serving container. In a small container, whisk together the olive oil, red wine vinegar, garlic, sugar, salt, and pepper. Toss the grain with some of the dressing, and reserve the rest for finishing.
2. When the grain has cooled, put in the basil, artichoke hearts, tomatoes, green onions, and mozzarella to the container and toss to blend. Put in more dressing if required. Place in your fridge the salad and any remaining dressing for maximum twelve hours. Take away the salad from the fridge half an hour before you serve and toss with additional dressing, if required.

Greek Salad With Grains and Lemon-Dill Vinaigrette

Ingredients:

- ¼ cup/30 g finely chopped fresh flat-leaf parsley
- ½ cup/110 g crumbled feta cheese
- ½ cup/120 ml extra-virgin olive oil
- ½ cup/85 g pitted Kalamata olives, crudely chopped
- 1 cup/155 g cherry tomatoes, halved, or quartered if large
- 1 cup/230 g finely diced unpeeled European or Asian cucumber
- 1 garlic clove, minced
- 1 Tbsp plus 1 tsp finely chopped fresh dill, or 2 tsp dried
- 3 cups/495 to 690 g freshly cooked grain of your choice
- Grated zest of 1 lemon, plus ¼ cup/60 ml fresh lemon juice
- Salt and freshly ground black pepper

Directions:

1. Place the warm grain in a big serving container. In a small container, whisk together the olive oil, red wine lemon zest, lemon juice, garlic, and dill. Sprinkle with salt and pepper if required. Toss the grain with some of the dressing, and reserve the rest for finishing.
2. When the grain has cooled, put in the cucumber, tomatoes, olives, feta, and parsley to the container and toss to blend. Put in more dressing if required. Place in your fridge the salad and any remaining dressing for

maximum twelve hours. Take away the salad from the fridge half an hour before you serve and toss with additional dressing, if required.

Italian Chickpea and Pasta Soup

Ingredients:

- ¼ cup/fifteen g finely chopped fresh flat-leaf parsley
- ½ cup/50 g ditali or another small pasta
- 1 medium onion, finely chopped
- 1 Tbsp extra-virgin olive oil
- 2 garlic cloves, minced
- 2 tsp finely chopped fresh rosemary
- 3 cups/720 ml chicken or vegetable broth
- Freshly grated Pecorino Romano cheese for decorate
- One 14½-oz/415-g can chopped tomatoes, with their juice
- Salt and freshly ground black pepper
- Two 14½-oz/415-g cans chickpeas, washed and drained

Directions:

1. Set a moderate-sized rice cooker to the regular cycle or to quick cook if using a fuzzy-logic machine. Warm the olive oil; put in the garlic, onion, and rosemary; and sauté for two to three minutes, or until the vegetables are translucent. Put in the tomatoes and sauté for

another two minutes. Put in 1 tsp salt, ½ tsp pepper, the chicken broth, chickpeas, and ditali.

2. Secure the lid and reset to the regular cycle. Set a timer for half an hour. Once the timer finishes, mix in the parsley and sprinkle with salt and pepper if required. Serve the soup in deep bowls, decorated with grated Pecorino Romano cheese.

Kitchen-Fresh Rice

Ingredients:

- ¼ cup/60 ml rice wine
- ¼ cup/60 ml tamari or soy sauce
- ½ cup/70 g bean sprouts
- ½ cup/85 g corn kernels cut from the cob, or frozen kernels, defrosted
- 1 celery rib, finely chopped
- 1 head baby bok choy, root end trimmed, leaves finely chopped
- 1 medium carrot, peeled and crudely grated
- 1 to 2 tsp toasted sesame oil
- 1 tsp grated peeled fresh ginger
- 2 big eggs, lightly beaten
- 2 cups/430 g long-grain rice
- 2 garlic cloves, minced

- 2 green onions, white and soft green parts, finely chopped
- 2 Tbsp vegetable oil
- 2½ cups/600 ml chicken or vegetable broth

Directions:

1. Put the rice in a sieve and wash under a stable stream of cool water, stirring the grains. Once the water appears to run clear, stop washing and shake the sieve to drain off surplus water.
2. Set a moderate-sized rice cooker to the regular cycle or to quick cook if using a fuzzy-logic machine. Heat 1 Tbsp of the vegetable oil; put in the garlic, ginger, carrot, and celery; and sauté for two to three minutes, or until the vegetables become tender. Put in the corn and rice and toast in the oil for a couple of minutes, tossing regularly. Gradually put in the tamari, rice wine, and chicken broth.
3. Secure the lid and reset to the regular cycle. While the rice is cooking, heat the rest of the 1 Tbsp oil in a small frying pan on moderate heat. Put in the eggs and cook until set on the bottom. Flip them and cook until set on the second side. Remove from the frying pan to a cutting board and chop the omelet into fine strips.
4. When the cooking cycle is complete, put in the bok choy and eggs to the rice, stirring to blend. Cover and carry on steaming for another three minutes on the keep-warm setting or with the machine turned off. If you own a

fuzzy-logic rice cooker, this will be taken care of automatically. Move the rice to a serving container or platter. Decorate using the bean sprouts and chopped green onions, sprinkle with a small amount of toasted sesame oil, before you serve.

Lemony Quinoa Salad With Tomato and Green Onions

Ingredients:

- ½ cup/120 ml extra-virgin olive oil
- 1 cup/155 g finely chopped tomatoes (out of season use cherry or pear tomatoes, quartered)
- 1 garlic clove, minced
- 1 Tbsp finely chopped shallot
- 1½ cups/280 g prewashed quinoa
- 2¼ cups/540 ml chicken or vegetable broth or water
- 3 celery ribs, finely chopped
- 3 green onions, white and soft green parts, finely chopped
- Freshly ground black pepper
- Grated zest of 2 lemons, plus 3 Tbsp fresh lemon juice
- Salt

Directions:

1. Mix the quinoa, chicken broth, 1 tsp salt, and half the lemon zest in a moderate-sized rice cooker. Close the lid and cook using regular cycle. When the cycle is complete, turn off the machine and allow the quinoa to carry on steaming for another five minutes. Move the quinoa to a big container and allow to cool.

2. In a small container, whisk together the olive oil, lemon juice, rest of the lemon zest, shallot, and garlic. Sprinkle with salt and pepper. Pour half the dressing over the cooled quinoa; reserve the rest for finishing. Fold in the tomatoes, celery, and green onions and lightly toss to blend. Place in your fridge the salad and any remaining dressing for maximum one day. Take away the salad from the fridge 1 hour before you serve and toss with additional dressing, if required.

Mediterranean Vegetable and Bulgur Stew

Ingredients:

- ¼ cup/30 g finely shredded Gruyère or imported Swiss cheese
- ¼ cup/fifteen g finely chopped fresh flat-leaf parsley
- ½ cup/105 g bulgur
- ½ cup/60 g freshly grated Parmigiano-Reggiano cheese
- ½ cup/80 g crudely chopped red bell pepper
- 1 medium red onion, finely chopped

- 1½ tsp herbes de Provence
- 2 cups/480 ml chicken or vegetable broth
- 2 garlic cloves, minced
- 2 Japanese eggplants, trimmed and finely chopped
- 2 small zucchini, trimmed and crudely chopped
- 2 Tbsp extra-virgin olive oil
- One 14½-oz/415-g can chopped tomatoes, with their juice
- Pinch of red pepper flakes
- Salt and freshly ground black pepper

Directions:

1. Put the bulgur in a sieve and wash under a stable stream of cool water, stirring the grains. Once the water appears to run clear, stop washing and shake the sieve to drain off surplus water.
2. Set a moderate-sized rice cooker to the regular cycle or to quick cook if using a fuzzy-logic machine. Heat the olive oil, put in the garlic and red pepper flakes, and sauté for half a minute, or until aromatic. Put in the onion and herbes de Provence and sauté for two to three minutes, until the onion starts to become tender. Put in the eggplants, bell pepper, and zucchini and sauté another three minutes to tenderize the vegetables. Put in the tomatoes and bulgur and stir until blended. Slowly put in the chicken broth.

3. Secure the lid and reset to the regular cycle. At the end of the cooking cycle, flavor the stew with salt and pepper if required. Mix in the parsley and serve the stew, decorated with the cheeses.

Nonna's Vegetable Soup

Ingredients:

- ¼ lb/115 g green beans, trimmed and slice into 1-in/2.5-cm pieces
- ⅓ cup/65 g lentils
- ½ cup/80 g finely chopped sweet yellow onion, such as Vidalia
- 1 cup/140 g finely chopped savoy cabbage, spinach, or black kale
- 1 cup/155 g canned crushed tomatoes, with their juice
- 1 medium carrot, peeled and finely chopped
- 1 medium zucchini, crudely chopped
- 1 tsp dried sage leaves
- 2 celery ribs, finely chopped
- 2 Tbsp extra-virgin olive oil
- 4 cups/960 ml chicken or vegetable broth

Directions:

1. Rind from Parmigiano-Reggiano cheese (approximately 1 in/2.5 cm square), cut into little dice (not necessary),

plus ⅓ cup/45 g finely shredded Parmigiano-Reggiano cheese

2. Salt and freshly ground black pepper
3. Set a moderate-sized rice cooker to the regular cycle or to quick cook if using a fuzzy-logic machine. Heat the olive oil; put in the onion, celery, carrot, and sage leaves; and sauté for about three minutes, or until the vegetables start to become tender. Put in the tomatoes, chicken broth, zucchini, green beans, cabbage, lentils, and Parmigiano rind (if using).
4. Secure the lid and set to the regular cycle. Set a timer for half an hour. Once the timer finishes, check the soup, and ensure the lentils are cooked. They should have split open and thickened the soup. Sprinkle with salt and pepper if required. Keep the soup warm until ready to serve. (If you would like a thinner soup, add a little extra broth or water, adjusting the seasonings accordingly.) Garnish each container of soup with shredded Parmigiano before you serve.

Red Beans and Rice

Ingredients:

- ½ cup/110 g long-grain rice
- ½ cup/80 g finely chopped celery
- ½ cup/80 g finely chopped green bell pepper

- ½ cup/80 g finely chopped sweet yellow onion, such as Vidalia
- ½ lb/225 g smoked sausage, cut into little dice
- 1 bay leaf
- 2 garlic cloves, minced
- 2 Tbsp extra-virgin olive oil
- 2 tsp dried thyme
- 3 cups/720 ml chicken or vegetable broth
- Assorted hot sauces for serving
- One 14½-oz/415-g can red beans, washed and drained
- Pinch of cayenne pepper
- Salt and freshly ground black pepper

Directions:

1. Put the rice in a sieve and wash under a stable stream of cool water, stirring the grains. Once the water appears to run clear, stop washing and shake the sieve to drain off surplus water.

2. Set a moderate-sized rice cooker to the regular cycle or to quick cook if using a fuzzy-logic machine. Heat the olive oil; put in the sausage, onion, garlic, celery, bell pepper, thyme, cayenne, and bay leaf; and sauté for two to three minutes, or until the vegetables become tender. Put in the red beans, rice, and chicken broth.

3. Secure the lid and reset to the regular cycle. Set a timer for half an hour. Once the timer finishes, check to ensure

the rice is soft. Flavour the red beans with salt and pepper, if required, and serve with assorted hot sauces.

Spring Vegetable Risotto

Ingredients:

- ⅓ cup/45 g freshly grated Parmigiano-Reggiano cheese
- ½ cup/120 ml dry white wine, such as Sauvignon Blanc or Pinot Grigio, or dry vermouth
- 1 cup/140 g packed baby spinach, finely chopped
- 1 cup/170 g shelled English peas
- 1 cup/170 g shelled fresh fava beans
- 1 cup/215 g medium-grain rice, such as Arborio, Carnaroli, or Vialone
- 1 fennel bulb, wispy ends removed and finely chopped
- 1 garlic clove, minced
- 1 leek, soft white part only, finely chopped
- 2½ cups/600 ml chicken broth
- 4 Tbsp/55 g unsalted butter
- Salt and freshly ground black pepper

Directions:

1. Put the rice in a sieve and wash under a stable stream of cool water, stirring the grains. Once the water appears to run clear, stop washing and shake the sieve to drain off surplus water.

2. Coat the interior of a moderate-sized rice cooker with nonstick cooking spray. Set the rice cooker to the regular cycle or to quick cook if using a fuzzy-logic machine. Melt 2 Tbsp of the butter; put in the garlic, leek, spinach, and fennel; and sauté for two to three minutes, or until the leek becomes tender. Put in the wine and bring to its boiling point. Put in the rice and chicken broth and stir to spread the ingredients.

3. Secure the lid and reset to the regular cycle. Set a timer for fifteen minutes. Once the timer finishes, mix in the fava beans and peas. Cover and allow to steam for another five minutes on the keep-warm setting or with the machine turned off. If you own a fuzzy-logic rice cooker, this will be taken care of automatically. Mix in the rest of the 2 Tbsp butter and the Parmigiano. Sprinkle with salt and pepper. Serve instantly.

Summer Squash Risotto

Ingredients:

- ¼ cup/30 g freshly grated Parmigiano-Reggiano cheese
- ½ cup/80 g finely chopped sweet yellow onion, such as Vidalia
- 1 cup/215 g medium-grain rice, such as Arborio or Carnaroli
- 1 medium yellow squash, finely diced

- 1 Tbsp extra-virgin olive oil
- 2 medium zucchini, finely diced
- 2 Tbsp finely chopped fresh mint
- 3 cups/720 ml chicken or vegetable broth
- 4 Tbsp/55 g unsalted butter

Directions:

1. Put the rice in a sieve and wash under a stable stream of cool water, stirring the grains. Once the water appears to run clear, stop washing and shake the sieve to drain off surplus water.
2. Set a moderate-sized rice cooker to the regular cycle or to quick cook if using a fuzzy-logic machine. Melt 2 Tbsp of the butter with the olive oil, put in the onion, and sauté for two to three minutes, or until the onion becomes tender. Put in the rice and toast for two to three minutes, stirring. Gradually put in the chicken broth.
3. Secure the lid and set to the regular cycle. Set a timer for fifteen minutes. Once the timer finishes, put in the zucchini and yellow squash. Cover and cook for another five minutes and then check to ensure the rice is firm to the bite (still firm to the bite). Mix in the mint and rest of the 2 Tbsp butter. Serve the risotto in shallow bowls, decorated with Parmigiano.

Summertime Grain Salad With Tomatoes, Zucchini, and Basil

Ingredients:

- ¼ cup/60 ml red wine vinegar
- ¼ cup/fifteen g packed basil leaves, thinly cut
- ½ cup/120 ml extra-virgin olive oil
- 1 cup/155 g cherry or pear tomatoes, halved, or quartered if large
- 1 medium zucchini, finely diced
- 3 cups/495 to 690 g freshly cooked grain of your choice
- 4 green onions, white and soft green parts, finely chopped
- Salt and freshly ground black pepper

Directions:

1. Place the warm grain in a big serving container. In a small container, whisk together the olive oil, red wine vinegar, 1 tsp salt, and ½ tsp pepper. Taste for seasoning and put in more salt and pepper if required. Toss the grain with some of the dressing, and reserve the rest for finishing.

2. When the grain has cooled, put in the tomatoes, green onions, zucchini, and basil to the container and toss to blend. Put in more dressing if required. Place in your fridge the salad and any remaining dressing for

maximum twelve hours. Take away the salad from the fridge half an hour before you serve and toss with additional dressing, if required.

Tomato-Parmesan Soup With Ricotta and Spinach Dumplings

Ingredients:

Soup

- 1 medium onion, finely chopped
- 2 garlic cloves, minced
- 2 medium carrots, peeled and finely chopped
- 2 Tbsp extra-virgin olive oil
- 2½ cups/600 ml chicken or vegetable broth
- One 14½-oz/415-g can crushed tomatoes, with their juices
- Rind from Parmigiano-Reggiano cheese (approximately 1 in/2.5 cm square), crudely chopped

Dumplings

- ¼ cup/fifteen g thinly cut fresh basil
- ½ cup/60 g freshly grated Parmigiano-Reggiano cheese
- ½ cup/60 g freshly shredded Parmigiano-Reggiano cheese

- ½ tsp freshly ground black pepper
- ¾ cup/185 g whole-milk ricotta cheese
- 1 big egg, lightly beaten
- 1 cup/55 g fresh bread crumbs
- 1 tsp salt
- 1/8 tsp freshly grated nutmeg
- 2 cups/280 g frozen chopped spinach, defrosted and meticulously drained

Directions:

1. ***TO MAKE THE SOUP:*** Set a moderate-sized rice cooker to the regular cycle or to quick cook if using a fuzzy-logic machine. Heat the olive oil; put in the garlic, onion, and carrots; and sauté until the onion becomes tender, two to three minutes. Put in the tomatoes, chicken broth, and Parmigiano rind. Secure the lid and reset to the regular cycle. Set a timer for half an hour.

2. ***TO MAKE THE DUMPLINGS:*** In a big container, mix the spinach, ricotta, grated Parmigiano, bread crumbs, egg, nutmeg, salt, and pepper, stirring until well mixed. Using a portion scoop, shape the dough into balls approximately 1 in/2.5 cm in diameter.

3. Once the timer finishes, cautiously put in the dumplings to the soup. Cover and cook for another ten minutes. Garnish each container of soup with some of the shredded Parmigiano-Reggiano and basil, before you serve.

Tuscan White Bean Soup With Rosemary and Pancetta

Ingredients:

- 1 cup/200 g small dried white beans, such as navy beans, soaked in cold water for 8 hours, washed, and drained
- 1 medium onion, finely chopped
- 2 celery ribs, crudely chopped
- 2 garlic cloves, minced
- 2 medium carrots, peeled and crudely chopped
- 2 Tbsp chopped fresh rosemary
- 2 Tbsp extra-virgin olive oil, plus more for drizzling
- 4 cups/960 ml chicken or vegetable broth, plus more if required
- One ½-in-/12-mm-thick slice pancetta, finely diced
- Salt and freshly ground black pepper

Directions:

1. Set a moderate-sized rice cooker to the regular cycle or to quick cook if using a fuzzy-logic machine. Heat the olive oil, put in the pancetta, and cook until crunchy. Put in the garlic, onion, and rosemary and sauté for two to three minutes to tenderize the onion. Put in the carrots, celery, and beans and stir until blended. Slowly put in the chicken broth.

2. Secure the lid and reset to the regular cycle. Set a timer for an hour. Check the beans from time to time to ensure that they are not clinging to the bottom of the pan. At the end of the hour, taste the beans to ensure they are tender and creamy; if not, set the timer for another fifteen minutes. Once the timer finishes, flavor the soup with salt and pepper if required. Serve the soup with a sprinkle of extra-virgin olive oil.

Umbrian Lentil Stew With Farro

Ingredients:

- ½ cup/100 g brown lentils, if possible small Italian ones
- ½ cup/100 g pearled farro
- 1 bunch celery with the leaves, tough outer stalks removed, crudely chopped
- 1 tsp dried sage leaves, crumbled in the palm of your hand
- 2 Tbsp extra-virgin olive oil
- 4 cups/960 ml chicken or vegetable broth, plus more if required
- Salt and freshly ground black pepper

Directions:

1. Put the farro in a sieve and wash under a stable stream of cool water, stirring the grains. Once the water appears

off surplus water.

2. Set a moderate-sized rice cooker to the regular cycle or to quick cook if using a fuzzy-logic machine. Heat the olive oil and sauté the celery and sage for two to three minutes, or until the celery is coated with the oil and starts to become tender. Put in the farro and lentils and stir until blended. Slowly put in the chicken broth.

3. Secure the lid and reset to the regular cycle. Set a timer for about twenty minutes. Once the timer finishes, ensure the stew has enough liquid and put in more broth if required. Continue cooking for about twenty minutes more; the stew must be thick but still have some liquid in the cooker. Flavour the stew with salt and pepper, if required, before you serve.

Vegetable Biryani

Ingredients:

- ¼ cup/fifteen g finely chopped fresh cilantro
- ½ lb/225 g green beans, trimmed and slice into 1-in/2.5-cm lengths
- 1 cup/160 g cauliflower florets, cut into 1-in/2.5-cm pieces
- 1 cup/170 g shelled English peas, or frozen petite peas, defrosted

- 1 cup/215 g basmati rice
- 1 cup/225 g sweet potato, peeled and finely chopped
- 1 medium red onion, finely chopped
- 1 tsp grated peeled fresh ginger
- 2 cups/480 ml chicken or vegetable broth
- 2 garlic cloves, minced
- 2 medium carrots, peeled and finely chopped
- 2 Tbsp vegetable oil
- 2 tsp Madras curry powder
- Assorted chutneys and lime pickles for serving
- Raita for serving

Directions:

1. Put the rice in a sieve and wash under a stable stream of cool water, stirring the grains. Once the water appears to run clear, stop washing and shake the sieve to drain off surplus water.

2. Set a moderate-sized rice cooker to the regular cycle or to quick cook if using a fuzzy-logic machine. Heat the vegetable oil; put in the garlic, ginger, and curry powder; and sauté for half a minute, or until aromatic. Put in the onion and sweet potato and stir to coat with the curry mixture. Put in the green beans, carrots, and rice and stir until blended. Gradually put in the chicken broth and cauliflower, stirring to blend.

3. Cover and reset the rice cooker to the regular cycle. At
    the end of the cooking cycle, mix in the peas. Allow the
    biryani to carry on steaming for another five minutes on
    the keep-warm setting or with the machine turned off. If
    you own a fuzzy-logic rice cooker, this will be taken care
    of automatically. Remove from the rice cooker, move to
    a platter, and decorate with the cilantro. Serve the
    biryani with the raita and assorted chutneys and lime
    pickles.

Endnote

Thank you for your time! I hope you found your new favorite rice cooker recipe in this book!